BROOK

The Open Door

Peter Brook was born in London and received his M.A. at Oxford, where he founded the Oxford University Film Society. He has been a director of the Royal Shakespeare Company and currently heads the International Centre of Theatre Research in Paris. He has directed over fifty productions, among them *Love's Labour's Lost*, *The Tempest*, and *King Lear* in Stratford-upon-Avon; *Ring Around the Moon*, *Oedipus*, *A View from the Bridge*, and *Hamlet* in London; *The Visit*, *Marat/Sade*, *A Midsummer Night's Dream*, and *The Tragedy of Carmen* in New York; *Sergeant Musgrave's Dance*, *The Conference of the Birds*, *Timon of Athens*, *The Mahabharata*, and *The Cherry Orchard*. Among the films he has directed are *Lord of the Flies*, *King Lear*, and *Meetings with Remarkable Men*. His operas include *The Marriage of Figaro* and *Boris Godunov* at Covent Garden, and *Faust* and *Eugène Onegin* at the Metropolitan Opera. His books include *The Empty Space* (1968) and *The Shifting Point* (1987).

The Open Door

The Open Door

Thoughts on Acting and Theatre

PETER BROOK

ANCHOR BOOKS

A Division of Random House, Inc.

New York

FIRST ANCHOR BOOKS EDITION, JANUARY 2005

Copyright © 1993 by Euro-Theatre Management Corporation

All rights reserved under International and Pan-American Copyright Conventions. Published in the United States by Anchor Books, a division of Random House, Inc., New York, and simultaneously in Canada by Random House of Canada Limited, Toronto. Originally published in the United States by Pantheon Books, a division of Random House, Inc., New York, in 1993.

Anchor Books and colophon are registered trademarks of Random House, Inc.

The Library of Congress has cataloged the Pantheon edition as follows:
Brook, Peter.
The open door : thoughts on acting and theatre / Peter Brook.
p. cm.
1. Theater. 2. Acting. 3. Drama. I. Title.
PN1655.B75 1993
792—dc20
93-18740

Anchor ISBN 1-4000-7787-7

Book design by Georgia Küng

www.anchorbooks.com

Printed in the United States of America
10 9 8 7 6 5 4 3 2 1

for Irina and Simon

Contents

The Slyness of Boredom   1

The Golden Fish   93

There Are No Secrets   117

The Slyness of Boredom

One day, in an English university, while giving the lectures that were the basis for my book *The Empty Space*, I found myself up on a platform in front of a big black hole, and right at the back of that hole I vaguely distinguished some people sitting in the darkness. As I began to speak, I felt that everything I said was quite pointless. I became more and more depressed, for I couldn't find a natural way of getting through to them.

I saw them sitting like attentive pupils, waiting for words of wisdom with which to fill their schoolbooks, while I was cast in the role of a tutor, vested with the authority that goes with standing six feet above the listeners. Luckily I had the courage to stop and suggest that we look for another space. The organisers went off, searched throughout the university and finally came up with a small room which was too narrow and very uncomfortable but where we found it possible to have a natural and more intense relationship. Speaking in these new conditions, I at once felt that a new contact existed between the students and myself. From that point on, I was able to talk freely and the audience was liberated in the same way. The questions, like the answers, flowed much more smoothly. The strong lesson concerning space that I received that day became the basis of the experiments that we undertook many years later in Paris, in our International Centre of Theatre Research.

In order for something of quality to take place, an empty space needs to be created. An empty space makes it possible for a new phenomenon to come to life, for anything that touches on content, meaning, expression, language and music can exist only if the experience is fresh and new. However, no fresh and new experience is possible if there isn't a pure, virgin space ready to receive it.

A remarkably dynamic South African director who created a Black Theatre movement in the South African townships said to me, "We have all read *The Empty Space,* it has helped us a lot." I was pleased but very surprised, as most of the book was written before our experiences in Africa and stant reference to the theatres of London, of Paris, New York . . . What could they have found of use in its text? How could they feel that the book was also for them? How could it link with the task of bringing theatre into the conditions of life in Soweto? I asked this question and he answered, "The first sentence!"

I can take any empty space and call it a bare stage. A man walks across this empty space whilst someone else is watching him, and this is all I need for an act of theatre to be engaged.

They had been convinced that doing theatre under their conditions was an unavoidable disaster because in the townships of South Africa there isn't a single "theatre building". They had the feeling they could not get very far if they didn't possess thousand-seat theatres, with curtains and flies, lights and coloured projectors, like in Paris, London and New York. Then suddenly along came a book the first sentence of which affirmed that they had all they needed for doing theatre.

In the early seventies we began doing experiments outside of what was regarded as "theatres". For the first three years we played hundreds of times in streets, in cafés, in hospitals, in the ancient ruins of Persepolis, in

African villages, in American garages, in barracks, between concrete benches in urban parks . . . We learned a lot, and the major experience for the actors was playing to an audience they could see, as opposed to the invisible audience to which they were accustomed. Many of them had worked in large, conventional theatres, and it was a profound shock to find themselves in Africa in direct contact with the audience, the only floodlight being the sun, which united spectator and performer in the same impartial glare. Bruce Myers, one of our actors, once said: "I've spent ten years of my life in the professional theatre without ever seeing the people for whom I'm doing this work. Suddenly I can see them. A year ago, I would have been panicked by the feeling of nakedness. The most important of my defences was being taken away. I'd have thought, 'What a nightmare to see their faces!' " Suddenly he realised that, on the contrary, seeing the spectators gave a new meaning to his work. Another aspect of the empty space is that the emptiness is shared: it's the same space for everyone who is present.

At the time I wrote *The Empty Space*, those who searched for a "Popular Theatre" believed that everything that was "for the people" automatically had vitality, as contrasted with something that didn't have vitality, which was called "Elite Theatre". At the same time, the "Elite" felt they were privileged participants in a serious intellectual adventure which contrasted strongly with the turgid and devitalised "Commercial Theatre". Meanwhile, those who were working on "Great Classic Texts" were convinced that "High Culture" injects into the veins of society a quality way beyond the low-grade adrenaline of a vulgar comedy. However, my experience over the years taught me that this is quite false and that a good space is one in which many varied energies converge and all those categories disappear.

Luckily, when I started working in the theatre I was totally ignorant of all classifications. The great advantage that England provided in those days was that there was no school, no master, no examples. The German theatre was totally ignored, Stanislavsky virtually unknown, Brecht just a name and Artaud not even that. There were no theories, so people doing theatre slid naturally from one genre to another. Great actors could go from performing Shakespeare to a farce or a musical comedy. The audience and the critics followed in all simplicity, without feeling that they—or "theatre art"—were being betrayed.

In the early fifties we presented *Hamlet* in Moscow with Paul Scofield, who had played major roles for over ten years or so and was known in England as one of the most brilliant and accomplished actors of his generation. This was in the old Stalinist Russia, completely isolated— in fact, I think we were the first English company to perform there. It was quite an event and Scofield was treated like a pop star.

Back in England, we continued to work together for a while, doing a play by Eliot, another by Graham Greene. One day, after our season had ended, he was offered the part of a cockney impresario in a musical comedy, the first of the pre-rock musicals. Paul was very excited: "It's wonderful. Instead of another Shakespeare play, I can sing and dance. It's called *Expresso Bongo*!" I encouraged him to accept, and he was very pleased and the play was a success.

While the show was running, an official Russian delegation comprised of about twenty actors, actresses, directors and theatre managers suddenly arrived from Moscow. As we had been so well received over there, I went to welcome them at the airport. The first question they asked concerned Scofield: "What's he doing? Can we see him?" "Of course," I replied. We arranged tickets for them and they went to see the show.

The Russians, especially in that period, had learned that one can always get out of any theatrical embarrassment with the use of one word: *interesting*. So they watched the play, met with Scofield and exclaimed unconvincingly that they had been "most interested". A year later we received a copy of a book written about the trip by the leader of the delegation, a Shakespeare expert at Moscow University. In the book I found a bad photo of Scofield wearing his slanting trilby from *Expresso Bongo*, with the following caption: "We were all saddened by the tragedy of the situation of the actor in a capitalist country. What humiliation for one of the greatest actors of our time to be forced to perform in something called *Expresso Bongo* in order to feed his wife and two children!"

I'm telling this story to share with you a fundamental idea: that theatre has no categories, it is about life. This is the only starting point, and there is nothing else truly fundamental. Theatre is life.

At the same time, one cannot say that there is no difference between life and theatre. In 1968 we saw people who, for very valid reasons, tired by so much "deadly theatre", insisted that "life is a theatre", thus there was no need for art, artifice, structures . . . "Theatre is being done everywhere, theatre surrounds us," they

2

said. "Each of us is an actor, we can do anything in front of anyone, it's all theatre."

What is wrong with this statement? A simple exercise can make it very clear. Ask any volunteer to walk from one side of a space to another. Anyone can do this. The clumsiest idiot cannot fail, he just has to walk. He makes no effort and deserves no reward. Now ask him to try to imagine that he is holding a precious bowl in his hands and to walk carefully so as not to spill a drop of its contents. Here again anyone can accomplish the act of imagination that this requires and can move in a more or less convincing manner. Yet your volunteer has made a special effort, so perhaps he deserves thanks and a five-penny piece as a reward for trying. Next ask him to imagine that as he walks the bowl slips from his fingers and crashes to the ground, spilling its contents. Now he's in trouble. He tries to act and the worst kind of artificial, amateur acting will take over his body, making the expression on his face "acted"—in other words, woefully unreal. To execute this apparently simple action so that it will appear as natural as just walking demands all the skills of a highly professional artist—an idea has to be given flesh and blood and emotional reality: it must go beyond imitation, so that an invented life is also a parallel life, which at no level can be distinguished from the real thing. Now we can see why a true actor is worth the enormous daily rate that film companies pay him for giving a plausible impression of everyday life.

One goes to the theatre to find life, but if there is no difference between life outside the theatre and life inside, then theatre makes no sense. There's no point doing it. But if we accept that life in the theatre is more visible, more vivid than on the outside, then we can see that it is simultaneously the same thing and somewhat different.

Now we can add some specifics. Life in the theatre is more readable and intense because it is more concentrated. The act of reducing space and compressing time creates a concentrate.

In life we speak in a chattering tumble of repetitive words, yet this quite natural way of expressing ourselves always takes a great deal of time in relation to the actual content of what one wants to say. But that is how one must begin—with everyday communication—and this is exactly like in theatre when one develops a scene through improvisation, with talk that is much too long.

The compression consists of removing everything that is not strictly necessary and intensifying what is there, such as putting a strong adjective in the place of a bland one, whilst preserving the impression of spontaneity. If this impression is maintained, we reach the point where if in life it takes two people three hours to say something, on stage it should take three minutes. We can see this result clearly in the limpid styles of Beckett, Pinter or Chekhov.

With Chekhov, the text gives the impression of having been recorded on tape, of taking its sentences from daily life. But there is not a phrase of Chekhov's that has not been chiseled, polished, modified, with great skill and artistry so as to give the impression that the actor is really speaking "like in daily life". However, if one tries to speak and behave just like in daily life, one cannot play Chekhov. The actor and the director must follow the same process as the author, which is to be aware that each word, even if it appears to be innocent, is not so. It contains in itself, and in the silence that precedes and follows it, an entire unspoken complexity of energies between the characters. If one can manage to find that, and if, furthermore, one looks for the art needed to conceal it, then one succeeds in saying these simple words and giving the impression of life. Essentially, it is life, but it is life in a more concentrated form, more compressed in time and space.

Shakespeare goes even farther. It used to be thought that verse was a form of beautifying through poetry. Then, as an inevitable reaction, came the idea that verse is no more than an enriched form of everyday speech. Of course, verse must be made to sound "natural", but this means neither colloquial nor ordinary. To find the way, one must see very clearly why the verse exists and what absolutely necessary function it has to perform. In fact, Shakespeare, as a practical man, was forced to use verse to suggest simultaneously the most hidden psychological, psychic and spiritual movements in his characters without losing their down-to-earth reality. Compression can hardly go farther.

The entire problem resides in trying to know if, moment for moment, in the writing or in the playing, there is a spark, the small flame that lights up and gives an intensity to that compressed, distilled moment. For compression and condensation are not enough. One can always reduce a play that's too long, too wordy, and still end up with something tedious. The spark is what matters, and the spark is rarely there. This shows to what extent the theatrical form is frighteningly fragile and demanding, for this small spark of life must be present each and every second.

This artistic problem exists only in the theatre and the cinema. A book may have its dull spots, but in the theatre, from one second to the next, the audience can be lost if the tempo is not right.

If I now stop speaking . . . we hear a silence . . . but everyone is paying attention . . . For a moment I have you in the palm of my hand, and yet in the next second your minds inevitably will wander. Unless . . . unless what? It is nearly superhuman to be able continually to renew the interest, find the originality, the freshness, the intensity, that each coming second demands. That is why, compared to other art forms, there exist so few masterpieces in the world's theatre. As the risk always exists that the spark of life will disappear, we must analyse precisely the reasons for its frequent absence. For this, one must observe the phenomenon with clarity.

Thus it is very important to examine simultaneously and without preference the classical theatre and the commercial theatre, the actor who rehearses for months and the one who prepares in a few days, comparing what is possible when there is a lot of money with what is possible when there is very little—in other words, all the different conditions in which acting takes place.

I wish to compare what can occur only on a regular stage, with a set and lighting, with what can take place only without lighting, without scenery, out of doors, in order to demonstrate that the phenomenon of a living theatre is not linked to external conditions. One can go and see a very banal play with a mediocre subject which is a huge hit and is making a great deal of money in a very conventional theatre, and sometimes find in it a spark of life quite superior to what happens when people spoon-fed on Brecht or Artaud, working with good resources, present a show that is culturally respectable but lacking in fascination. Faced with this type of performance, one can quite easily spend a dreary evening watching something in which everything is present—except life. It is very important to appraise this coldly, clearly, pitilessly, especially if one wishes to avoid being influenced by the snobbery of so-called cultural criteria.

That is why I insist on the dangers that represent a very great author such as Shakespeare, or great works of opera. The cultural quality of these pieces can bring out the best or the worst. The greater the work, the greater the dreariness if the execution and interpretation is not of the same level.

This is always very difficult to admit for those who have been struggling, often with difficulty, to find the means to bring work of a serious cultural level to an indifferent audience. One is nearly always forced to defend the attempt, and we are frequently very disappointed because audiences, in every country, often refuse these works and prefer what we consider to be of lower quality. If one looks carefully, one notices the weakness. The great work, the masterpiece, is in fact presented without the one ingredient that can link it to its audience: the irresistible presence of life. Which brings us back to the empty space.

If habit leads us to believe that theatre must begin with a stage, scenery, lights, music, armchairs . . . we set off on the wrong track. It may be true that to make films one needs a camera, celluloid and the means to develop it, but to do theatre there is only one thing one needs: the human element. This does not mean that the rest is unimportant, but it is not the primary concern.

I once claimed that theatre begins when two people meet. If one person stands up and another watches him, this is already a start. For there to be a development, a third person is needed for an encounter to take place. Then life takes over and it is possible to go very far— but the three elements are essential.

For example, when two actors play together in a rehearsal, without an audience, there is the temptation for them to believe that theirs is the only relationship that exists. They can then be trapped into falling in love with the pleasure of a two-way exchange, forgetting that a three-way exchange is what it's all about. Too much time in rehearsal can end by destroying the unique possibility which the third element brings. The moment we feel that a third person is watching, the conditions of a rehearsal are always transformed.

In our work we often use a carpet as a rehearsal zone, with a very clear purpose: off the carpet, the actor is in daily life, he can do what he wants—waste his energy, engage in movements that don't express anything in particular, scratch his head, fall asleep . . . But as soon as he finds himself on the carpet, he is under the obligation of having a clear intention, of being intensely alive, simply because an audience is watching.

I have tried the following experiment in front of an audience: asking two people chosen at random to come up and just say "Hello!" to one another. Then I turn to the audience and ask if this is the most remarkable thing they have ever seen. Obviously it isn't.

Next I put it to the audience: Can we say that those five seconds were filled with such purity, such quality, possessing such elegance and subtlety at every moment that they are unforgettable? Could you, the audience swear that for the rest of your life this scene will remain indelible in your memory? Only if you can answer yes, and if at the same time you can also say that "it seemed quite natural", only then can you consider what you have just seen a theatrical event. So what was lacking? This is the crux of the matter. What is needed to take the ordinary towards the unique?

In the Nô theatre, an actor will take five minutes to reach the centre of the stage. How is it that a "non-actor" cannot hold our attention, while a "real actor" doing the same thing two thousand times more slowly can be so compelling? Why, when we watch him, will we be touched, fascinated? Better yet, why should a great Nô master be even more riveting in his walk than a lesser Nô actor with only a quarter of a century of practise behind him? What is the difference?

We are speaking of the simplest of movements—walking—yet there is a fundamental difference between what leads to an intensity of life and that which is merely commonplace. Any detail within a movement will serve our purpose; we can put it under the microscope of our attention and observe the entire simple process.

The eye of the audience is the first element which helps. If one feels this scrutiny as a true expectation which demands at every moment that nothing be gratuitous, that nothing can come from limpness, but all from alertness, one understands then that the audience does not have a passive function. It does not need to intervene or manifest itself in order to participate. It is a constant participant through its awakened presence. This presence must be felt as a positive challenge, like a magnet before which one cannot allow oneself to be "any-old-how". In the theatre, "any-old-how" is the great and subtle enemy.

Daily life consists of being "any-old-how". Let us take three examples. For instance, if one is taking an exam, or when one speaks with an intellectual, one will endeavour not to be "any-old-how" in thought or in speech, but without realising it, "any-old-how" will be in our body, which will be ignored and limp. However, if we are with someone who is in distress, we will not be "any-old-how" in our feelings, we will certainly be kind and attentive, but our thoughts may be adrift or confused, and the same with our bodies. And in the third case, when one is driving a car, the entire body may well be mobilised, but the head, left to itself, can drift into "any-old-how" thoughts.

For an actor's intentions to be perfectly clear, with intellectual alertness, true feeling and a balanced and tuned body, the three elements—thought, emotion, body—must be in perfect harmony. Only then can he fulfil the requirement to be more intense within a short space of time than when he is at home.

In our earlier experiment—"a person moves through a space and meets a second person while another watches"—there is a potential which may or may not be realised. To understand this in terms of an art, we will need to see very precisely what elements create this mysterious movement of life—and which ones prevent it from appearing. The fundamental element is the body. In all the races on our planet, the bodies are more or less the same; there are a few differences in size and colour, but essentially the head is always above the shoulders, the nose, eyes, mouth, stomach and feet are in the same places. The instrument of the body is the same throughout the world, what differs are the styles and cultural influences.

Japanese children have infinitely more developed bodies than those in the West. From the age of two, a child learns to sit in a perfectly balanced manner; between two and three the child begins to bow regularly, which is a wonderful exercise for the body. In the hotels in Tokyo, very attractive young girls stand all day in front of the lifts and bow each time the lift doors open and close. If one of these girls were one day chosen by a director to do theatre, you can be sure that at least her body would be well developed.

In the West, among the few people who at the age of

eighty have perfectly developed and attuned bodies are orchestra conductors. All his life, a conductor, without considering it an exercise, makes movements that begin with the bending of the torso. Like the Japanese, he needs a solid stomach so that the rest of his body can make particularly expressive movements. These are not the movements of an acrobat or a gymnast, which originate in tension, but movements in which emotion and precision of thought are linked. He requires this precision of thought to follow every detail of the score, while his feelings give quality to the music and his body, in permanent motion, is the instrument through which he communicates to the players. Thus the aged conductor enjoys a perfectly supple body, even though he doesn't perform the dances of a young African warrior, or the bows of the Japanese.

A great English conductor from the turn of the century stated that "on the Continent conductors are better prepared because, when they meet a lady, they bow to kiss her hand". He advised all aspiring conductors to bow and kiss the hand of all the ladies they should meet.

When I took my daughter, then three or four years old, to a dance class, I was appalled by the state of the bodies of the children. I could see children of her age already stiff, without rhythm. Rhythm is not a particular gift. Everyone has rhythm in him until it is blocked, and at the age of three, one should move naturally. But to-day's children, spending hours motionless in front of a television set, go to dance classes with bodies that are already rigid. The instrument that is the body is not as well developed with us during childhood as in the East. So a Western actor must realise that he needs to compensate for these deficiencies.

This does not mean that an actor must train like a dancer. An actor must have a body that reflects his type, whereas a dancer's body may well be neutral. Dancers—I speak now of traditional ballet, of classical dance—have to be able to follow the indications of the choreographer in a relatively anonymous manner. It is different for the actor; it is very important for an actor to be physically conspicuous, to make an image of the world; there must be small fat ones, tall thin ones, those who glide quickly, others who lumber heavily . . . This is necessary because it is life that we are showing, inner and outer life, each inseparable from the other. To have an expression of outer life, one must have strongly marked types, as each of us represents a certain type of man or woman. But it is important—and this is where the link with the Eastern actor lies—that the body that is fat and clumsy and the one that is young and quick must be equally fine in their sensitivity.

When our actors do acrobatic exercises, it is to develop sensitivity and not acrobatic ability. An actor who never does any exercise "acts from the shoulders up". Although this may serve him well in films, it does not enable him to communicate the totality of his experience in the theatre. It is in fact very easy to be sensitive in language or in the face, or in the fingers, but what is not given by nature and must be developed through work is this same sensitivity in the rest of the body, in the back, the legs, the rear. Sensitive means that the actor is at all times in contact with his entire body. When he initiates a movement, he knows the exact place of every limb.

In the *Mahabharata* we did a scene that was extremely dangerous; it took place in the dark, with everyone carrying burning torches. The sparks and the drops of boiling oil could easily have set fire to the flowing scarves of the thin silk costumes. We were terrified each time by the risk involved. As a result, we frequently did exercises with torches so that each of us would know where the flames were at any given moment. From the beginning the Japanese actor Yoshi Oida was the most qualified because of his rigorous training. Whatever movement he executes, he knows exactly where he has placed his feet, his hands, his eyes, the angle of his head . . . He does nothing by chance. But if you ask the average actor suddenly to stop in the middle of a movement and to tell you, to within a centimetre, where his foot or his hand is, he will often have the greatest of difficulties. In Africa or in the East, where children's bodies are not warped by city life, and where a living tradition compels them day after day to sit up right, bow, kneel, walk discreetly, stand motionless but alert, they already possess what for us must be acquired through a series of exercises. This is perfectly possible, however, because the structure of the bodies is similar.

An untrained body is like an untuned musical instrument—its sounding box is filled with a confusing and ugly jangle of useless noises that prevent the true melody from being heard. When the actor's instrument, his body, is tuned by exercises, the wasteful tensions and habits vanish. He is now ready to open himself to the unlimited possibilities of emptiness. But there is a price to pay: in front of this unfamiliar void there is, naturally, fear. Even when one has had long experience performing, each time one starts again, as one finds oneself on the edge of the carpet, this fear—of emptiness in oneself, and of emptiness in the space—reappears. At once one tries to fill it so as to get away from the fear, so as to have something to say or do. It takes real confidence to sit still or to stay silent. A large part of our excessive, unnecessary manifestations come from a terror that if we are not somehow signaling all the time that we exist, we will in fact no longer be there. This is a bad enough problem in daily life, where nervous, overexcited people can drive us up the wall, but in the theatre, where all energies must converge on the same aim, the ability to recognise that one can be totally "there", apparently "doing" nothing, is supremely important. It is important for all actors to recognise and identify such obstacles, which in this case are both natural and legitimate. If one were to ask a Japanese actor about his playing, he would acknowledge that he has faced and crossed this barrier. When he acts well, it comes not from having previously built a mental construction, but from having made a panic-free emptiness within.

In a village in Bengal, I watched a very powerful ceremony called the Chauu. The participants, people from the village, act out battles, moving forward in little jumps. They stare in front of themselves as they jump, and there is in their gaze an incredible strength, an unbelievable intensity. I asked their teacher, "What do they do? On what are they concentrating to have such a powerful look?" He answered: "It's very simple. I ask them to think of nothing. Just to look forward and keep their eyes wide open." I realised that this intensity would never have come if they had been concentrating on: "What am I feeling?" or if they had filled the space with ideas. This is hard for the Western mind to accept, having turned "ideas" and the mind into supreme deities for so many centuries. The only answer is in direct experience, and in the theatre one can taste the absolute reality of the extraordinary presence of emptiness, as compared with the poverty-stricken jumble in a head crammed with thinking.

What are the elements that disturb the inner space? One of them is excessive reasoning. So why does one insist on preparing things? It is nearly always to fight against the fear of being caught out. In the past I knew conventional actors who liked to be given every directorial detail on the first day of rehearsal and not be bothered anymore. This was absolute heaven for them, and if you wished to modify some detail two weeks before the opening, they would get very upset. As I like to change everything, sometimes even on the day of a performance, I can no longer work with that kind of actor, if he or she still exists. I prefer to work with actors who enjoy being flexible. But even with them, some will occasionally say,

"No, it's too late, I can't change anything anymore," purely because they are frightened. They are convinced that, having erected a certain structure, if it's taken away they will be left with nothing, that they will be lost. In those cases, there's no point saying to them "Don't worry," as this is the most certain way of frightening them even further. Quite simply, you have to show them that it's not true. Only precise and repeated rehearsal and performance experiences will permit you to demonstrate to an actor that if one doesn't search for security, true creativity fills the space.

So we come to the question of the actor as artist. One can say that a true artist is always ready to make any number of sacrifices in order to reach a moment of creativity. The mediocre artist prefers not to take risks, which is why he is conventional. Everything that is conventional, everything that is mediocre, is linked to this fear. The conventional actor puts a seal on his work, and sealing is a defensive act. To protect oneself, one "builds" and one "seals". To open oneself, one must knock down the walls.

The question goes very far. What one calls "building a character" is in fact fabricating a plausible counterfeit.

So one must find another approach. The creative approach is to fabricate a series of temporary counterfeits, knowing that even if one day you feel you have discovered the character, this cannot last. On any particular day it may be the best you can do, but you must remember that the true form is not yet there. True form only arrives at the last moment, sometimes even later. It is a birth. True form is not like the construction of a building, where each action is the logical step forward from the previous one. On the contrary, the true process of construction involves at the same time a sort of demolition. This means accepting fear. All demolitions create a dangerous space in which there are fewer crutches and fewer supports.

At the same time, even when one achieves moments of true creativity, in improvisation, in rehearsal or during a performance, there always exists the danger of blurring or destroying the emerging form.

Let us use the example of audience reaction. If during an improvisation you feel the presence of the people watching you—which you must, otherwise it makes no sense—and those people laugh, you risk being pulled by that laughter in a direction that you wouldn't necessarily have taken without hearing the laughter. You wish to please, and the laugh confirms to you that you are succeeding, so you begin to focus more and more on getting laughs, until your links with truth, reality and creativity dissolve invisibly in the merriment. The essential is to be aware of this process and not be trapped blindly. In the same way, if you are conscious of what provokes fear, you can observe how you set up your defences. All the elements that give security need to be observed and questioned. A "mechanical actor" will always do the same thing, so his relationship with his partners can be neither subtle nor sensitive. When he watches or listens to the other players, it is only a pretence. He hides in his "mechanical" shell because it gives him security.

It is the same for the director. There is a great temptation for a director to prepare his staging before the first day of rehearsal. This is quite natural and I always do it myself. I make hundreds of sketches of the scenery and the movements. But I do this merely as an exercise, knowing that none of it is to be taken seriously the next day. This doesn't hold me back, it is a good preparation— but if I were to ask actors to apply the sketches that I did three days or three months earlier, I would kill everything that can come to life at the moment of the rehearsal. One needs to do the preparation in order to discard it, to build in order to demolish . . .

It is a fundamental rule that until the last moment, everything is a form of preparation, so one must take

risks, bearing in mind that no decision is ever irrevo-
cable.

One of the inherent and in-
evitable aspects of an empty space is the absence of scenery. This does not mean that it is better, for I am not
passing judgment, but simply stating the obvious, that
in an empty space there cannot be any scenery. If there
is scenery, the space is not empty, and the mind of the
spectator is already furnished. A naked area does not
tell a story, so each spectator's imagination, attention
and thought process is free and unfettered.

In these circumstances, if two people move across the
space and one says to the other, "Hello! Mr. Livingstone,
I presume," these words are sufficient to conjure up
Africa, palm trees, and so on. If, on the other hand, he
had said, "Hello . . . where is the Metro?" the spectator
would visualize a different set of images and the scene
would be a street in Paris. But if the first person says,
"Where is the Metro?" and the second person answers,
"The Metro? Here? In the middle of Africa?" several
possibilities open up, and the image of Paris forming in
our mind begins to dissolve. Either we are in the jungle
and one of the characters is crazy, or we are in a street

in Paris and the other character is having delusions. The absence of scenery is a prerequisite for the functioning of the imagination.

If all you do is place two people side by side in an empty space, each detail comes into focus. For me, this is the great difference between theatre in its essential form and cinema. With cinema, because of the realistic nature of photography, a person is always in a context, never a person outside a context. There have been attempts to make films with abstract settings, without scenery, with white backdrops, but apart from Dreyer's *Jeanne d'Arc*, this has seldom worked. If one considers the thousands of great films that have been made, one can see that the strength of cinema lies in photography, and photography involves somebody being somewhere. In that way, cinema cannot for a moment ignore the social context in which it operates. It imposes a certain everyday realism in which the actor inhabits the same world as the camera. In the theatre, one can imagine, for example, an actor in his everyday clothes indicating that he is playing the pope by wearing a white ski hat. One word would be sufficient to conjure up the Vatican. In the cinema this would be impossible. One would need a specific explanation in the story, such as its taking place in an asylum and the patient with the white hat having

31

delusions about the church, without which the image could not make sense. In the theatre, the imagination fills the space, whereas the cinema screen represents the whole, demanding that everything in the frame be linked in a logically coherent manner.

Emptiness in the theatre allows the imagination to fill the gaps. Paradoxically, the less one gives the imagination, the happier it is, because it is a muscle that enjoys playing games.

If we talk about "audience participation" what do we mean? In the sixties we dreamed of an audience "participating". Naïvely, we thought that participating meant demonstrating with one's body, jumping onto the stage, running around and being part of the group of actors. Indeed, everything is possible and this kind of "happening" can sometimes be quite interesting, but "participation" is something else. It consists in becoming an accomplice to the action and accepting that a bottle becomes the tower of Pisa, or a rocket to the moon. The imagination will happily play this kind of game on condition that the actor be "nowhere". If behind him there is one single element of scenery to illustrate "spaceship" or "Manhattan office", a cinematographic plausibility immediately intervenes and one is locked into the logical confines of the set.

In an empty space, we can accept that a bottle is a rocket and that it will take us to meet a real person on Venus. A fraction of a second later it can change both in time and space. It is enough for an actor to ask, "How many centuries have I been here?" and we make a giant leap forward. The actor can be on Venus, then in a supermarket, go backwards and forwards in time, return to being the narrator, take off again in a rocket and so on within a few seconds with the help of a minimum number of words. This is possible if we are in a free space. All conventions are imaginable, but they depend on the absence of rigid forms.

The experiments we made in this area began in the seventies with what we called *The Carpet Show*. During our travels, to Africa and other parts of the world, all we would take with us was a small carpet that defined the area on which we would work. It was through this that we experienced the technical basis of Shakespearean theatre. We saw that the best way to study Shakespeare was not to examine reconstructions of Elizabethan theatres, but simply to do improvisations around a carpet. We realised that it was possible to begin a scene standing, end it by sitting down, and in standing up again find oneself in another country, at another time, without losing the tempo of the story. In Shakespeare, there are scenes where two people are walking in an enclosed space and suddenly find themselves in the open without any noticeable break. One part of the scene is indoors, another outdoors, without any indication of the point at which the transition occurs.

Several Shakespeare specialists have written volumes on this subject, frequently raising the question of his use of "double time". "How is it that this great author did not notice his mistake when at one point in his text he says an action has lasted three years, at another point a year and a half and in reality only two minutes," they ask. "How could this clumsy writer have written his first sentence indicating that we are "inside", and in the following sentence write something like "Look at this tree", which implies that we are in a forest?" It is surely obvious that Shakespeare was writing theatre for an infinite space within undefined time.

One is not bound by a unity of place, a unity of time, when the emphasis is on human relationships. What holds our attention is the interplay between one person and another; the social context, always present in life, is not shown but is established by the other characters. If the relationship between a rich woman and a thief is the subject of the action, it is neither the set nor the props that create this relationship but the story, the action itself. He is a thief, she is rich, along comes a judge: the human relationship between the woman, the thief and the judge creates the context. The setting, in the living sense of the word, is created in a dynamic and totally free manner by the interaction of the characters. The entire "play", including the text and all its social and political implications, will be the direct expression of the underlying tensions.

If one finds oneself in a realistic set, with a window for the thief to climb through, a safe to crack, a door for the rich lady to open . . . then cinema can do it better! In conditions that imitate ordinary life, the rhythm will have the flabbiness of our basic daily activities, and it is here that the editor of a film steps in, using his scissors to cut away all the bits of movement that are of no interest. The filmmaker has an advantage which the theatre director will acquire only if he leaves the realistic set and turns to the open stage. Then theatre, *by being theatrical*, comes to life again. This brings us back to our starting point: for there to be a difference between theatre and non-theatre, between everyday life and theatrical life, there needs to be a compression of time that is inseparable from an intensification of energy. This is what creates a strong link with the spectator. This is why, in most forms of village and popular theatre, music plays an essential role in raising the energy level.

Music begins with a beat. The simple presence of a pulse or a throb is already a tightening of the action and a sharpening of the interest. Then other instruments enter to play more and more sophisticated roles—always in relation to the action. I need to stress this point. Music in theatre—as popular forms have always recognised pragmatically—only exists in relation to the performing energies. It has no connection at all with the stylistic questions that belong to the mainstream of composed music as it evolves, school by school, over the centuries. This is something very easy for a performing musician to understand, provided that he is interested in following and developing the energies of an actor. It is, however, very hard for a composer to accept this. I am not in any way attacking composers, only explaining how for many years we have found that a musical form intimately related to the actors' work has come from performing musicians who from the start have been an integral part of the group's activities. Of course, a composer can make magnificent contributions, but only if he recognizes that he must enter into the unified language of the performance, not by trying to appeal to the spectator's ear in a separate language of his own.

The theatre is perhaps one of the most difficult arts, for three connections must be accomplished simultaneously and in perfect harmony: links between the actor and his inner life, his partners and the audience.

First, the actor must be in a deep, secret relationship with his most intimate sources of meaning. The great storytellers I've seen in teahouses in Afghanistan and Iran recall ancient myths with much joy, but also with inner gravity. At every moment they open themselves to their audiences, not to please them, but to share with them the qualities of a sacred text. In India, the great storytellers who tell the *Mahabharata* in the temples never lose contact with the grandeur of the myth that they are in the process of reliving. They have an ear turned inwards as well as outwards. This is as it should be for every true actor. It means being in two worlds at the same time.

This is very difficult and complex, and leads to the second challenge. If he plays Hamlet or King Lear and is listening to the response to myth in the most hidden areas of his psyche, he must still be completely in touch with the other actors. One part of his creative life, at the moment he performs, must be turned inwards. Can he do this truly—100 percent—without ever letting it cut him off, even for a moment, from the person standing before him? This is so incredibly difficult that this is where there is the greatest temptation to cheat. One often sees actors, sometimes very great actors—and opera singers above all—conscious of their reputation, totally involved with themselves and only pretending to play with their partner. This immersion in themselves can't be written off simply as vanity or narcissism. On the contrary, it can come from a profound artistic concern, which unfortunately does not go as far as to totally include the other person. A Lear will pretend to play with his Cordelia, with a very skillful imitation of looking and listening, but in fact he is only concerned with being a polite partner, which is very different from being one of a duo creating a world together. If he is just the disciplined fellow actor, partly switched off when it's not his turn, he cannot be faithful to his major obligation, which is to hold a balance between his external behaviour and his most private impulses. Almost always, something is neglected, except in moments of grace when there is no tension, no subdivisions, when the ensemble acting is seamless and pure.

In the rehearsal period one must take care not to go too far too soon. Actors who exhibit themselves emotionally too early on often become incapable of finding true relationships with one another. In France I had to stress this because of the readiness of many actors to plunge immediately into the joys of letting themselves go. Even if the text is written so as to be spoken strongly, we often need to begin by rehearsing in the greatest intimacy, so as not to dissipate our energy. However, where the actors are in the habit of beginning huddled around a table, protected by scarves and cups of coffee, it is, on the contrary, vital to liberate the creativity of the whole body by movement and improvisation. To be sufficiently free to feel a relationship, it is often useful to improve a text with other words, other movements. But of course, all this is a temporary passage, made to reach that very difficult and elusive thing which consists of keeping in touch with one's intimate content whilst simultaneously speaking with a loud voice. How does one allow this intimate expression to grow until it can fill a vast space without betrayal? How does one raise the pitch of one's voice without it distorting the relationship? It is incredibly difficult: it is the paradox of acting.

As if the two challenges I have spoken of are not difficult enough, we must now consider the third obligation. The two actors who are performing must at the same time be both characters and storytellers. Multiple storytellers, storytellers with many heads, for at the same time as they are playing an intimate relationship between themselves, they are speaking directly to the spectators. Lear and Cordelia are not only interrelating as truthfully as possible as king and daughter, but as good actors they must also sense that the audience is being carried along with them.

So one is permanently forced to struggle to discover and maintain this triple relationship; to one's self, to the other and to the audience. It is easy to ask the question "How?" There is no comforting recipe to be given. A triple balance is a notion that at once throws up the image of a tightrope walker. He recognises the dangers, he trains to be ready to face them, but the balance is there to be found or lost each time he steps on the wire.

The greatest guiding principle I know of in my work, the one to which I always pay the most attention, is boredom. In the theatre, boredom, like the slyest of devils, can appear at any moment.

The slightest thing and he jumps on you, he's waiting and he's voracious. He is always ready to slip invisibly into an action, a gesture or a sentence. Once one knows this, all one needs is to trust one's own built-in capacity to be bored and use this as a reference, knowing that it is what one has in common with all the beings on Earth. It's extraordinary; if during a rehearsal or an exercise I say to myself, "If I'm bored, there must be a reason for it," then, out of desperation, I have to look for the reason. So I give myself a jolt and out comes a new idea— which jolts the other person, who jolts me back. As soon as boredom appears, it is like a flashing red light.

Of course, each person has a different boredom quotient. What one must develop in oneself has nothing to do with restlessness or a poor attention span. The boredom I am speaking about is the sense of no longer being held riveted in the unfolding action.

For many years at our Centre in Paris we have created a tradition which has become very important to us. About two-thirds of the way through the rehearsal period, we go and perform the work in progress, just as it is, unfinished, before audiences. Usually we go to a school and we play to an unprepared audience of children: in most cases they do not know the play and have not been told what to expect. We go without props, without costumes, without staging, improvising with whatever objects we can find in the "empty space" that the classroom provides.

One cannot do this at the beginning of rehearsals, everyone is too frightened, closed and unprepared— which is quite natural—but once a good deal of real work has taken place, we are in a position to try out what we have discovered in order to see where we touch an interest in people other than ourselves, and where we merely provoke boredom. An audience made up of children is the best of critics; children have no preconceptions, they are interested immediately or instantly bored, and they either go along with the actors or they get impatient.

When one reaches the eventual audience, the great barometer is in the levels of silence. If one listens carefully one can learn everything about a performance from the degree of silence it creates. Sometimes a certain emotion ripples through the audience and the quality of the silence is transformed. A few seconds later and one can be in a completely different silence, and so on, passing from a moment of great intensity to a moment less intense, when the silence will inevitably weaken. Someone will cough, or fidget, and as boredom settles in, it will express itself through small noises, through a person shifting his weight, so that the springs of his seat creak and the hinges squeak, or, worst of all, the sound of a hand opening the programme.

Thus, one must never pretend that what one is doing is automatically interesting, and never say to oneself that the audience is bad. It is true that there are sometimes very bad audiences, but one must rigorously refuse to say so, for the simple reason that one can never expect an audience to be good. There are only easy audiences and less easy ones, and our job is to make every audience good. When the audience is easy, it is a gift from heaven, but a difficult audience is not an enemy. On the contrary, an audience is by its very nature resistant, and one must always be looking for what can excite and transform its level of interest. This is the healthy basis of the commercial theatre, but the real challenge arises when the aim is not success, but the arousing of intimate meanings without trying to please at all costs.

In a proscenium theatre, when the rehearsals occur without any audience contact, the day the curtain rises for the first time, there is no reason for there to be a pre-established contact between the audience and those on stage who are presenting the story. The show often begins at a certain pace, and the audience is not in the same tempo. When a play fails on its opening night, one can see that the actors have their rhythm, that each member of the audience has his own rhythm, and that all these disparate movements never harmonise with each other.

In village theatre, on the other hand, from the first drumbeat, the musicians, actors and audience share the same world. They are in unison. The first movement, the first gesture creates the link, and from that point onwards, all the development of the story takes place through a common rhythm. We have experienced this often, not only during our experiments in Africa, but also when playing in community halls, gymnasiums and other spaces. It gives a clear impression of the relationship which must come about and on what the rhythmic structure of a show depends. Once one becomes aware of this principle, one understands more clearly why it is that a play in the round, or in any non-proscenium space where the audience surrounds the actors, often has a naturalness and a vitality quite different from what a frontal, picture-frame theatre can offer.

The reasons a play is put on are usually obscure. In justification one says, "Such a play was chosen because our taste, or our beliefs, or our

cultural values demand that we put on this type of play."
But for what reason? If one doesn't ask that one question,
then thousands of subsidiary reasons can appear: the
director wants to show his conception of the play, there
is an experiment in style to demonstrate, a political theory to illustrate . . . Thousands of imaginable explanations, but secondary when compared to the underlying
issue: Can the theme succeed in touching an essential
preoccupation or need in the audience?

Political theatre, when not played to the already con-
verted, often stumbles at this hurdle, but nothing illus-
trates it so clearly as when a traditional show is taken
out of its context.

When I first went to Iran in 1970, I saw a very powerful
form of theatre known as Ta'azieh. Our little group of
friends had come a long way across Iran, by air to Mash-
had, and then by taxi deep into the rolling, open coun-
tryside, off the one main road and down a muddy track
to keep an improbable rendezvous with a theatre performance. Then suddenly we were outside a brown wall
that circumscribed the village, where near a tree two
hundred villagers made a circle. Standing and sitting in
the scorching sun, they made a ring of humanity so complete that we five outsiders were totally absorbed into
their unity. There were men and women in traditional

dress, young men in jeans leaning on their bicycles, and children everywhere.

The villagers were in perfect expectation, because they knew down to the last detail what was to come, and we, knowing nothing, were a sort of perfect audience. All we had been told was that the Ta'azieh is the Islamic form of a mystery play, that there are many such plays, and that they deal with the martyrdom of the first twelve imams who followed the prophet. Although banned by the shah for many years, they continued to be performed in clandestinity in three or four hundred villages. The one we were about to see was called *Hossein*, but we knew nothing about it: not only did the idea of an Islamic drama suggest nothing, but it even awoke a doubting corner of the mind to remind us that Arab countries have no traditional theatre because representation of the human form is forbidden by the Koran. We knew that even the walls of mosques were decorated with mosaics and calligraphies instead of the huge heads and searching eyes found in Christianity.

The musician sitting under the tree struck a rhythm insistently on his drum and a villager stepped into the circle. He was wearing his rubber boots and had a fine courageous air. Around his shoulders he carried a length of bright green cloth, the sacred colour, the colour of fertile land, which showed, so we were told, that he was a holy man. He began to sing a long melodic phrase made up of a very few notes in a pattern that repeated and repeated, with words that we could not follow but whose meaning became instantly clear through a sound that came from deep inside the singer. His emotion was in no way his own. It was as though we heard his father's voice, and his father's father's, and so on back. He stood there, his legs apart, powerfully, totally convinced of his function, and he was the incarnation of that figure that for our theatre is always the most elusive one of all, the hero. I had long doubted that heroes could be depicted: in our terms, the heroes, like all good characters, easily become pallid and sentimental, or wooden and ridiculous, and it is only as we go toward villainy that something interesting can begin to appear. Even as I was saying this to myself, another character, this time with a red twist of cloth about him, entered the circle. The tension was immediate: the bad one had arrived. He did not sing, he had no right to melody, he just declaimed in a strong rasping tone, and then the drama was underway.

The story became clear: the imam was safe for the present but he had to travel farther. But to do so, he would have to pass through the lands of his enemies, who were already preparing an ambush. As they snarled and shouted out their evil intentions, fear and dismay rippled through the spectators.

Of course, everyone knew that he would make the journey, and everyone knew he would be killed, but at first it seemed as though somehow today he could avoid his fate. His friends argued with him not to go. Two small boys singing in unison, his sons, came into the circle and passionately begged him not to leave. The martyr knew the fate that awaited him. He looked at his sons, sang a few poignant words of farewell, clasped them to his chest and then strode away, his big farmer's boots carrying him firmly across the ground. The boys stood watching him leave, their lips trembling. Suddenly it was too much for them and they ran after him, throwing themselves on the ground at his feet. Again they repeated an entreaty in the same high musical phrase. Again he answered with his melody in farewell, again he clasped them, again he left them, again they hesitated, and then again they ran, even more intensely, to throw themselves once more at his feet, as again the same melody was repeated . . . Again and again, back and forth across the circle, the identical scene was repeated. By the sixth time, I became aware of a low murmur all around me, and taking my eyes for a moment off the action, I saw lips trembling, hands and handkerchiefs stuck in mouths, faces wrought with paroxysms of grief and then the very old men and women, then the children and then the young men on bicycles all began sobbing freely.

Only our tiny group of foreigners remained dry-eyed, but fortunately we were so few that our lack of participation could do no harm. The charge of energy was so powerful that we could not break the circuit, and so we were in a unique position as observers close to the heart of an event of an alien culture, without bringing to it any disturbance or distortion. The circle was operating according to certain very fundamental laws and a true phenomenon was occurring, that of "theatrical representation". An event from the very distant past was in the process of being "re-presented", of becoming present; the past was happening here and now, the hero's decision was for now, his anguish was for now and the audience's tears were for this very moment. The past was not being described nor illustrated, time had been abolished. The village was participating directly and totally, here and now in the real death of a real figure who had died some thousand years before. The story had been read to them many times, and described in words, but only the theatre form could work this feat of making it part of a living experience.

This is possible when there is no attempt to pretend

that any element be more than it is. Consequently there is no vain perfectionism. From a certain point of view, perfectionism can be seen to be homage and devotion— man's attempt to worship an ideal that is linked to his pushing his craftsmanship and artistry to its limit. From another point of view, this can be seen as the fall of Icarus, who tried to fly above his station and reach the gods. In the Ta'azieh there is no attempt, theatrically speaking, to do anything too well: the acting does not demand characterisations that are too complete, detailed or realistic. If there is no attempt to embellish, there is in its place another criterion: the need to find the true inner echo. Clearly this cannot be an intellectual or consciously prepared attitude, but in the sound of the voices was the unmistakeable ring of great tradition. The secret was clear. Behind this manifestation was a way of life, an existence that had religion as its root, all-present and all-penetrating. What in religion is so often an abstraction, a dogma or a belief became here the reality of the villagers' faith. The inner echo does not come from faith: faith arises within the inner echo.

A year later, when the shah was trying to give the world a good liberal image of his country, it was decided to present the Ta'azieh to the world at the next Shiraz International Festival of the Arts. So naturally this first international Ta'azieh would have to be the best of all Ta'aziehs. Scouts were sent off around the country to pick out the finest elements. Eventually actors and musicians from widely scattered villages were rounded up and brought together in Teheran, measured and fitted by costumiers, drilled by a professional theatre director, coached by a conductor and then bundled off by motor coach to perform in Shiraz. Here, in the presence of the queen and five hundred international festival guests in gala evening dress, totally indifferent to the sacred content, the villagers were put, for the first time in their lives, on a platform facing front, with spotlights blazing down on them through which they could dimly perceive a bank of society figures, and they were expected "to do their stuff". The rubber boots worn by the village shopkeeper, in which he had looked very smart, had been replaced by leather ones, a lighting designer had prepared lighting effects, the temporary props had been replaced with well-made ones, but no one had stopped to ask what "stuff" they were expected to do. And why? And for whom? These questions were never put, because no one was interested in the answers. So the long trumpets hooted, the drums played, and it meant absolutely nothing.

The spectators, who had come to see a pretty piece of

folklore, were delighted. They did not realise that they
had been conned and that what they had seen was not a
Ta'azieh. It was something quite ordinary, rather dull,
devoid of any real interest, and which gave them nothing.
They didn't realise this because it was presented as "culture", and at the end the officials smiled and everyone
happily followed them towards the buffet.

The *embourgeoisement* of the show was total, but
the most lugubrious and unwatchable aspect, the most
"deadly", was that audience. The whole tragedy of official cultural activities was epitomised in that one evening. It is not only a Persian problem, it is the same
wherever well-meaning bodies try charitably, peering
downwards from on top, to preserve a local culture and
then share it with the rest of the world. It dramatises
more than anything the most vital and least considered
element of the theatre process: the audience. Because
the meaning of Ta'azieh starts not with the audience at
the performance, but with the way of life experienced by
that audience. This way of life is permeated with a religion which teaches that Allah is everything and in
everything. And this is the ground on which everyday
existence rides, this religious sense pervades everything.
So the daily prayers or the yearly play are only different

forms of the same thing. Out of this essential unity can come a totally coherent and necessary theatre event. But the audience is the factor that makes the event alive. As we saw, it could absorb outsiders, provided they were in a tiny proportion to the mass of the audience. When the nature and motivation of the audience changed, the play lost all of its meaning.

The same phenomenon occurred in London during the Festival of India, with the Bengal Chauu of which I spoke earlier. In India it is performed at night, with music, noises, extraordinary whistles, and the village children hold burning torches to light up the performance. All through the night the village is in an incredible state of excitement, the people jump around, there is a great acrobatic sequence where they leap over the screaming children, and so on. This time, however, the Chauu were performing at the Riverside Theatre, a good space, but it was at tea-time, before an audience of about fifty elderly ladies and gentlemen, subscribers to Anglo-Indian periodicals, who were interested in the East. They politely watched the performance that had just arrived in London via Calcutta. Although this time there had been no smartening-up, no director, and the actors were doing exactly the same thing as in their village, the spirit was no longer present, nothing was left but a show, a show with nothing to show.

T his brings me to a choice which always remains open. If one wants to touch the spectator strongly, and with his help open up a world that is linked to his world yet at the same time makes it richer, larger, more mysterious than the one which we see day to day, there are two methods.

The first consists in searching for beauty. A great part of Oriental theatre is based on this principle. For the imagination to be amazed, one searches in every element for the greatest beauty. Let us take for example the Kabuki in Japan, or the Kathakali in India: the attention given to the makeup, the perfection of the smallest prop is all for reasons that go beyond pure aestheticism. It's as if through the purity of detail, one were trying to go towards the sacred. Everything in the set, the music and the costumes is made to reflect another level of existence. The slightest gesture is studied to eliminate from it the banal and the vulgar.

The second method, which is diametrically opposed, starts from the notion that an actor possesses an extraordinary potential for creating a link between his own imagination and the imagination of the audience, with the result that a banal object can be transformed into a magical one. A great actress can make one believe that an ugly plastic water bottle held in her arms in a certain way is a beautiful child. One needs an actor of high quality to bring about the alchemy where one part of the brain sees a bottle, and the other part of the brain, without contradiction, without tension, but with joy, sees the baby, the parent holding the child and the sacred nature of their relationship. This alchemy is possible if the object is so neutral and ordinary that it can reflect the image that the actor gives to it. It could be called an "empty object".

What our group from the International Centre has searched for over the years are ways of understanding which of these conditions corresponds best with what each subject demands. When we played Jarry's anarchic and satirical farce *Ubu Roi*, its form, even in our Paris theatre, came from a wild energy and free improvisations. We decided to tour through France in the least "magical" of spaces, so we found ourselves in a series of school halls, gymnasiums, sports complexes, each uglier and more unwelcoming than the last. For the actors, the exciting task was momentarily to transform these uninviting places and make them glow with life, so the key to this work was "roughness"—a seizing of crudeness with both hands. This suited one specific project but cannot be applied to all plays nor to all conditions. However, when a transformation takes place, impurity becomes the greatest glory of the theatre, beside which a pious search for purity seems woefully naïve.

True questions are often found in paradox and are impossible to resolve. There is a balance to be found between that which tries to be pure and that which becomes pure through its relationship to the impure. One can thus see to what extent an idealistic theatre cannot exist as long as it attempts to be outside the rough texture of this world. The pure can only be expressed in theatre through something that in its nature is essentially impure. We must remember that theatre is made by people and executed by people through their only available instruments, human beings. So the form is in its very nature a mixture where pure and impure elements can meet. It is a mysterious marriage that is at the centre of legitimate experience, where private man and mythical man can be apprehended together within the same instant of time.

In *The Empty Space* I wrote that a form, once created, is already moribund. What this means is hard to express, so I will try to give concrete examples.

When in 1968 I met our Japanese actor Yoshi Oida for the first time, he said to me: "I was educated in Japan in Nô theatre, I had a Nô master. I have worked in Bunraku and in Nô, but I feel that this magnificent form is not truly in touch with life today. If I stay in Japan, I will not be able to find a solution to this problem. I have a great deal of respect for what I have learned, but at the same time I need to look elsewhere. I have come to Europe with the hope of finding a means for breaking away from this form, which although magnificent does not speak sufficiently to us today. Another form must exist."

His conclusion was so deeply felt that it changed the form of his life: a magnificent form is not necessarily the appropriate vehicle to carry a living experience once the historical context changes.

The second example is from an experience I had during *The Conference of the Birds*. I have always hated masks, which for me are inherently deadly. However, for this play it seemed interesting to reopen the question, and we found a group of Balinese masks that are very close to human features and yet miraculously free of the morbid associations of a death mask. We invited a Balinese actor,

Tapa Sudana, to work with us. The first day he showed everybody how one performs with the mask, how each character has a very precise series of movements that the mask dictates and which are now fixed by tradition. The actors watched with interest and respect, but they soon realised that none of them were capable of doing what Tapa illustrated. He used the mask as in Balinese tradition, with a thousand years of ritual behind it. It would have been ridiculous for us to try to be what we were not. We finally asked him what it was possible for us to do.

"For the Balinese, what really matters is the moment when one puts on the mask," he said. This was no longer a stylistic indication, but an essential one. "We take the mask, and for a long time we look at it, until we feel the face so strongly that we can begin to breathe with it. It is only at that point that we put it on." From that moment, each of us tried to find his own relationship to the mask, through observing and feeling its nature, and it was a surprising experience to see that outside of the coded gestures of Balinese tradition, there were a thousand forms and a thousand new movements that corresponded to the life of the mask. This was suddenly within the reach of all of us, because it did not go through the codes frozen by tradition. In other words, we had broken the form and a new one had risen spontaneously and naturally like a phoenix from the ashes.

The third example I can give is the first demonstration I ever saw of Kathakali dancing, which took place in a California drama school. The demonstration was split into two parts. In the first part the dancer was made up and in costume, and he performed a traditional Kathakali dance under the conditions of a real performance, with recorded music and so on. It was very beautiful and very exotic. When we returned after the interval, the actor had removed his makeup. He was wearing jeans and a shirt and began to give explanations. To bring life to his explanations, he would demonstrate, playing the characters but without being forced to make the exact, traditional gestures. Suddenly this new simpler, more human form became infinitely more eloquent than the traditional one.

Generally speaking, we can conclude that *tradition*, in the sense we use the word, means "frozen". It is a frozen form, more or less obsolete, reproduced through automatism. There are a few exceptions, such as when the quality of the old form is so extraordinary that even today life remains in it, in the way that some very old people remain incredibly alive and touching. However, all form is deadly. There is no form, beginning with ourselves, that is not subject to the fundamental law of the universe: that of disappearance. All religion, all understanding, all tradition, all wisdom accepts birth and death.

Birth is a putting into form, whether one is speaking about a human being, a sentence, a word or a gesture. It is what the Indians call *sphota*. This ancient Hindu concept is magnificent because its actual meaning is already there in the sound of the word. Between the unmanifest and the manifest, there is a flow of formless energies, and at certain moments there are kinds of explosions which correspond to this term: "*Sphota!*" This form can be called an "incarnation". Some insects only last for a day, some animals several years, humans last longer and elephants last even longer. All these cycles exist, and it is the same thing with an idea or with a memory.

There is in all of us a memory that is a form. Some forms of memory, such as "Where did I park my car?" last for hardly a day. You go and see an idiotic play or film and the next day you cannot remember what it was about. At the same time, there are other forms that last much longer.

When one puts on a play, inevitably, at the beginning

it has no form, it is just words on paper or ideas. The event is the shaping of the form. What one calls the work is the search for the right form. If this work is successful, the result can eventually last for a few years, but no more. When we did our own version of *Carmen*, we gave it a completely new form which lasted four or five years before we felt it had reached its limit. The form no longer had the same energy: its time quite simply was up.

This is why one must not confuse virtual form with realised form. The realised form is what one calls a show. It takes its external form from all the elements that are present at its birth. The same play put on today in Paris, in Bucharest or in Baghdad will obviously be very different in form. The locale, the social and political climate, the prevailing thought and culture must all have their influence on what makes a bridge between a subject and the audience, what affects people.

I am sometimes asked what is the relation between the *Tempest* that I did thirty years ago in Stratford and the one I put on recently at the Bouffes du Nord. This question is absolutely ridiculous! How would it be possible for there to be the slightest resemblance of form between a play put on in another period, in another country, with actors who were all of the same race, and today's version, created in Paris with an international company, two Japanese, an Iranian, Africans . . . who bring such different understandings to the text and who have lived together through so many varied experiences.

The form need not be something invented by the director alone, it is the *sphota* of a certain mixture. This *sphota* is like a growing plant that opens up, lasts its time, wilts, then yields its place to another plant. I insist strongly on this because there exists a big misunderstanding which frequently blocks work in the theatre, and which consists in believing that what the author or the composer of the play or opera once wrote on paper is a sacred form. We forget that the author, when writing dialogue, is expressing hidden movements deeply buried in human nature, that when he writes stage directions, he is proposing production techniques based on the play-houses of his day. It is important to read between the lines. When Chekhov describes an interior or an exterior in great detail, what he is really saying is: "I want it to look real." After his death, a new form of theatre—the open arena stage—came into existence, one which Chekhov had never known. Since then many productions have demonstrated that the three-dimensional, cinematic relationships of the actors with minimal props and furniture on an empty stage seems infinitely more real, in a Chekhovian sense, than the cluttered picture sets of the proscenium theatre.

We are also touching here on the great misunderstanding about Shakespeare. Many years ago it used to be claimed that one must "perform the play as Shakespeare wrote it". Today the absurdity of this is more or less recognised: nobody knows what scenic form he had in mind. All that one knows is that he wrote a chain of words that have in them the possibility of giving birth to forms that are constantly renewed. There is no limit to the virtual forms that are present in a great text. A mediocre text may only give birth to a few forms, whereas a great text, a great piece of music, a great opera score are true knots of energy. Like electricity, like all sources of energy, energy itself does not have a form, but it has a direction, a power.

In any text, a structure exists, but no true poet thinks *a priori* about this structure. Although he has integrated in himself certain rules, there is a very intense impulse which pushes him to make certain meanings come to life. In trying to make these elements live, he runs into the rules, and it is at that point that it integrates itself into a structure of words. Once it is printed, the form becomes a book. If we are speaking of a poet or a novelist, this will suffice. But for the theatre, one is only halfway there. What is written and printed does not yet have dramatic form. If we say to ourselves: "These words must be pronounced in a certain manner, have a certain tone or rhythm . . ." then, unfortunately, or maybe fortunately, we will always be mistaken. It leads to everything that is so awful in tradition, in the worst sense of the term. An infinite quantity of unexpected forms can appear from the same elements, and the human tendency to refuse the unexpected always leads to the reduction of a potential universe.

We are now at the heart of the problem. Nothing exists in life without form: we are forced at each instant, especially when speaking, to look for form. But one must realise that this form may be the absolute obstacle to life, which is formless. One cannot escape from this difficulty, and the battle is permanent: the form is necessary, yet it is not everything.

Faced with this difficulty, there is no point adopting a purist attitude and waiting for the perfect form to fall from the heavens, for in that case one would never do anything at all. This attitude would be stupid. Which brings us again to the question of purity and impurity. The pure form does not come down from the sky. The putting into form is always a compromise that one must accept whilst at the same time saying to oneself: "It's temporary, it will have to be renewed." We are touching here on a question of dynamics which will never end.

When we started to work on *Carmen*, the only thing on which we agreed was that the form given by Bizet was not necessarily what he would have given it today. We had the impression that Bizet had been like a Hollywood screenwriter hired today by a major studio to make an epic movie from a very beautiful story. The screenwriter, who knows the rules of the game, accepts that he is forced to take into account the criteria of commercial cinema, an argument repeated to him each day by his producer. We had the feeling that Bizet had been profoundly touched by reading Mérimée's tale, which is an extremely sparse novella with a style rigorously without ornamentation, without complications, without artifice, at the opposite pole from the flourishes of a baroque author. It is very simple and very short. Though basing his work on this novella, Bizet was forced to make an opera for his period, for a particular theatre, the Opéra Comique, where there were, as in Hollywood today, particular conventions that had to be observed, such as colorful scenery, choruses, dances and processions. We agreed with one another that *Carmen* is often very boring in performance and we tried to discover the nature of this boredom and its causes. We came to the conclusion that, for example, a stage suddenly invaded by eighty people who sing and then leave without reason was profoundly boring. So we asked whether a chorus was really necessary to tell Mérimée's story.

Then, sacrilegiously, we confessed to ourselves that the music was not consistently of the same quality. What was quite exceptional was the music which expressed the relationships between the protagonists, and we were struck by the fact that it was into these musical lines that Bizet had poured his deepest feelings and his finest sense of emotional truth. Thus we made the decision to see if we could extract from the four hours of the full score what we deliberately called the *Tragedy of Carmen*, referring to the concentrated interrelation of a small number of protagonists in Greek tragedy. In other words, we cut all decoration so as to preserve the strong and tragic relationships. We felt that here could be found the finest passages of music, which could only be appreciated in intimacy. When an opera is put on in a big theatre, on a large scale, it may have vitality and vivacity, but not necessarily a very great quality. We looked for music which could be sung softly, lightly, without excess and without exhibitionism, without great virtuosity. By doing that, by moving towards intimacy, we were essentially searching for quality.

Earlier I spoke of boredom as my greatest ally. Now I would like to advise you that each time you go to the theatre and you are bored, not to hide it, not to believe that you are the guilty party, that it is your fault. Do not let yourselves be truncheoned by the beautiful idea of "culture". Ask yourself the question: "Is there something missing in me or in the show?" You have the right to challenge this insidious idea, socially accepted today, that "culture" is automatically "superior". Naturally, culture is something very important, but the vague idea of culture that is not re-examined, renewed, is an idea used like a truncheon to prevent people from making legitimate complaints.

What is even worse is that culture is becoming considered like a fancy car or the "best" table in a good restaurant, as an exterior sign of social success. This is the basic concept of corporate "sponsoring". The principle of the "sponsor" is a miserable one. The only fundamental motivation for a sponsor of a theatrical occasion is to have an event to which he can bring his clients. This has its own logic, and as a consequence the performance must conform to the idea they have of culture: that it be prestigious and reassuringly boring.

The Almeida, a small theatre in London with a very good reputation, wanted to bring over our *Tragedy of Carmen*. The management had asked for financial support from a large bank, which was delighted to participate. "*Carmen*—what a wonderful idea!" Once all the preparations for the trip had been made, the manager of the theatre received a phone call from the person in charge of cultural events for the bank: "I have just received your brochures, it's strange . . . your theatre is not in the heart of London? It's on the outskirts? And *Carmen* is to be performed by four singers and two actors? The orchestra is reduced to fourteen musicians? And the chorus? There isn't a chorus!?! But who do you think we are? Do you imagine that this bank will take its best customers to the suburbs to see *Carmen* without a chorus and with a reduced orchestra?" And he hung up. We never played in London.

This is why I insist on the difference between a culture that is alive and this other extremely dangerous side of culture that is beginning to pervade the modern world, especially since the spread of this relationship between show and sponsor. This does not mean that we do not need sponsors. As government support dwindles all over the world, sponsorship is the only alternative; theatre cannot remain dynamic and adventurous if it depends uniquely on the box office. But the sponsors must be enlightened. Luckily, in our work, we have had some admirable support, so we know that they can exist. However, it is a matter of luck: enlightenment can't be taught, though it must always be encouraged when it appears.

As it is the business of business people to be cunning, one must be ready to outwit them at their own game. When years ago I did *King Lear* on American T.V., there were four sponsors, which meant four commercial breaks. I suggested to them that if they voluntarily refrained from interrupting Shakespeare, this would get them far more publicity. In fact, at the time this was so surprising that editorials were even written to salute their integrity. That trick could only work once. Each time one must think up something new.

I am constantly asked to explain what I meant when I wrote in *The Empty Space* about two theatres, "Holy" and "Rough", coming together in a form I called "Immediate". Regarding "Holy Theatre", the essential thing is to recognise that there is an invisible world which needs to be made visible. There are several layers of invisible. In the twentieth century we know only too well the psychological layer, this obscure area between what is expressed and what is concealed. Nearly all contemporary theatre recognises the great Freudian underworld where, behind the gesture or the words, can be found the invisible zone of the ego, the super-ego and the unconscious. This level of psychological invisibility has nothing to do with sacred theatre. "Holy Theatre" implies that there is something else in existence, below, around and above, another zone even more invisible, even farther from the forms which we are capable of reading or recording, which contain extremely powerful sources of energy.

In these little-known fields of energy exist impulses which guide us towards "quality". All human impulses towards what we call in an imprecise and clumsy manner "quality", come from a source whose true nature we entirely ignore but which we are perfectly capable of recognising when it appears either in ourselves or in another person. It is not communicated through noise but through silence. Since one must use words, one calls it "sacred". The only question that matters is the following: Is the sacred a form? The decline, the decadence of religions comes from the fact that one confuses a current, or a light, neither of which has a form, with ceremonies, rituals and dogmas, which are forms that lose their meaning very swiftly. Certain forms which were perfectly adapted for certain people for a few years, or for an entire society over the course of a century, are still with us today, defended with "respect". But of what respect are we speaking?

For thousands of years, man has realised that nothing is more terrible than cultivating idolatry, because an idol is only a piece of wood. The sacred is either present at all times, or it doesn't exist. It is ridiculous to think that the sacred exists at the top of the mountain and not in the valley, or on a Sunday or the Sabbath and not the other days of the week.

The problem is that the invisible is not obliged to make itself visible. Although the invisible is not compelled to manifest itself, it may at the same time do so anywhere, and at any moment, through anyone, as long as the conditions are right. I don't think there is any point in reproducing the sacred rituals of the past which are not very likely to bring us towards the invisible. The only thing which may help us is an awareness of the present. If the present moment is welcomed in a particularly intense manner, and if conditions are favourable for a *sphota*, the elusive spark of life can appear within the right sound, the right gesture, the right look, the right exchange. So, in a thousand very unexpected forms, the invisible may appear. The quest for the sacred is thus a search.

The invisible may appear in the most everyday objects. The plastic water bottle or the scrap of cloth of which I spoke earlier may be transformed and impregnated by the invisible, provided that the actor is in a state of receptivity and that his talent is equally refined. A great Indian dancer could make sacred the most mundane of objects.

The sacred is a transformation, in terms of quality, of that which is not sacred at the outset. Theatre is based on relationships between humans who, because they are human, are by definition not sacred. The life of a human being is the visible through which the invisible can appear.

The "Rough Theatre", popular theatre, is something else. It is the celebration of all sorts of "available means" and carries with it the destruction of everything that has to do with aesthetics. This does not mean that beauty does not enter into it, but the "Rough" are those who say: "We have no outside means, not a penny, no craftsmanship, no aesthetic qualifications, we can pay neither for beautiful costumes nor for sets, we have no stage, we have nothing other than our bodies, our imaginations and the means at hand."

When in our travels the International Centre group was working with *The Carpet Show* I spoke of earlier, it was precisely with such available means. In many countries it was interesting to note that we found ourselves in the same tradition as the groups of popular theatre that we met, because in fact we were not looking for tradition. In the most diverse locations, we found that the Eskimos, the Balinese, the Koreans and ourselves were doing exactly the same thing. I knew a wonderful theatre company in India, a village theatre full of very talented and inventive people. If they had to perform a play here today, they would immediately have used the cushions on which you are seated, this bottle, this glass, these two books . . . because those are the available means. That is the essence of "Rough Theatre".

I went on in *The Empty Space* to speak about "Immediate Theatre". This was to underline that everything I had said until then was very relative. One must not take anything in the book as a dogma, nor as being a definitive classification, everything is subject to chance and change. In fact, "Immediate Theatre" suggests that, whatever the subject matter, one must find the best means, here and now, to bring it to life. One can see right away that this demands a permanent, case-by-case exploration, depending on the needs. Once one realises this, all questions of style and convention explode, because they are limitations, and one finds oneself before an extraordinary richness, because everything is possible. The means of the Sacred Theatre are just as available as are the means of the Rough Theatre. Immediate Theatre can thus be defined as the "Whatever It Needs Theatre", that is to say, a theatre in which the purest and the most impure elements can each find their legitimate place. The example, as always, is in Shakespeare.

We are touching again on the conflict between two necessities: that of an absolute freedom in the approach, the recognition of the fact that "everything is possible", and, on the other hand, the strictness and the discipline which insist that the "everything" is not just "anything".

How does one situate oneself between the "everything is possible" and the "anything is to be avoided." Discipline in itself may be either negative or positive. It may close all the doors, deny freedom, or, on the other hand, constitute the indispensable rigour needed to emerge from the morass of the "anything". That is why there are no recipes. Staying too long in the depths can become boring. Staying too long in the superficial soon becomes banal. Staying too long on the heights may be intolerable. We must move all the time.

The great eternal question that we ask ourselves is: "How are we to live?" But great questions remain completely illusory and theoretical if there isn't a concrete base for application in the field. What is wonderful is that the theatre is precisely the meeting place between the great questions of humanity— life, death—and the craftlike dimension, which is very practical, as in pottery. In the great traditional societies, the potter is someone who tries to live with great eternal questions at the same time he is making his pot. This double dimension is possible in the theatre; it is, in fact, what gives it all its value.

Maybe we are preparing a production and we begin to think about the setting. This simple and basic question is a very practical one: "Is it good or not? Does it perform a function? Does it work?" If one takes as a starting point an empty space, then the only question is that of efficiency. Is the empty space insufficient? If the answer is yes, then one starts to consider what the indispensable elements are. The basis of the craft of the shoemaker is to make shoes that don't hurt; the basis of theatre craft consists in producing, with the audience, from very concrete elements, a relationship that works.

Let us try to approach this in another manner through the question of improvisation. For a long time now everybody uses the word, it is one of the clichés of our period, everywhere people are "improvising". It is useful to note that the word covers millions of possibilities, both good and bad.

Be warned, however, that in certain cases even the "any-old-how" is good! On the first day of rehearsals, it is virtually impossible to invent something stupid—that is, really stupid—because even the flimsiest idea can be useful if it gets people on their feet and into action. I will say, perhaps, the first thing that comes into my head: "Stand up, take the cushion on which you are seated and quickly change places!"

This is very easy, fun, better than sitting nervously on a chair, so everyone follows this childish proposition with enthusiasm. Then I can develop it: "Starting again much more quickly, without bumping into each other, in silence . . . calmly . . . form a circle!"

You see, one can invent anything. I said the first thing that came to mind. I did not ask myself: "Is this stupid, very stupid or too stupid?" I did not pass the slightest judgment on my own idea at the moment when it appeared. So very soon the atmosphere becomes more relaxed, and we all know each other better. We are thus ready to move on to something else. In this way, some exercises are useful, like games, simply because they relax. But they wear thin very fast, and an intelligent actor will soon resent being treated like a child. So the director has to be ahead of him and can no longer think off the top of his head. He now must make propositions that contain the real challenges and are useful to the work, such as exercises that make him struggle with those parts of his organism that are the most lethargic, or those areas of his emotional world that relate to the themes of the play, yet which he is afraid to explore. So why improvise? First, to create an atmosphere, a relationship, to make everybody comfortable, to allow each and every one to stand up, to sit, without it becoming an ordeal. As fear is inevitable, the first need is trust. And since what frightens people most of all today is speaking, one must begin neither with words, nor ideas, but with the body. A free body is where it all lives or dies. Let us at once put this into practise. We'll start from the notion that anything—almost anything—that gets our energies flowing cannot fail to be useful. So don't let's search for anything extraordinary. Let's do something together and if it seems foolish, what does it matter? So, stand up and make a circle! There are cushions on the ground, so each one take a cushion, throw it in the air and catch it . . .

Now that you've tried it, you see you can't go wrong, and as you're laughing together, already you feel a little bit better. However, if we just go on throwing cushions aimlessly, our enjoyment will fade and we'll soon wonder where this is leading us. To hold our interest, a new challenge must be found. So let us now introduce a tiny difficulty. Throw the cushion in the air, spin around on yourself and catch it! Again, it's enjoyable, because as we miss and drop the cushions we become determined to do better next time. And if we increase the tempo, throwing and spinning faster and faster, or spinning several times within each throw, our excitement increases.

Now, very rapidly, you find that you are nearly in control of this movement, so again a further element must be added. Throw your cushion in the air, move over to your right, catch the cushion of your neighbour, and try to keep the circle rotating smoothly, with less panic, less wasted movement.

Now it's not quite so easy, but we will not push this exercise to perfection. Let us just note that we are a bit more animated and the body is warming up. However, we can't pretend that there is a true rigour in what we are doing. As in many improvisations, the first step is important, but it is not sufficient. One must be very conscious of the many traps that are in what we call theatre games and exercises. With the possibility of using one's body more freely than in daily life, a feeling of joy appears very quickly, but if there isn't at the same time a real difficulty, the experience leads nowhere. This goes for all forms of improvisation. Often theatre groups who improvise regularly apply the principle of never interrupting an improvisation that is under way. If you really want to know what boredom is, watch an improvisation where two or three actors get going and "do their thing" without being stopped. They inevitably find themselves very rapidly repeating clichés, often with a deadly slowness that lowers the vitality of everyone watching. Sometimes the most challenging improvisation need only last a matter of seconds, like Sumo wrestling, for in this style of Japanese combat the aim is clear, the rules are strict but everything is decided in the lightning improvised choices made by the arms and legs in the very first moments.

I'm now going to suggest to you a new exercise, but first a word of warning: do not try to reproduce what we are doing here in another context. It would be a tragedy if next year in drama schools all over the place, young actors started throwing cushions into the air on the pretext that it's a "Famous Exercise from Paris". There are much more amusing things to invent.

Now, all fifteen of you sitting in the circle count out loud, one after the other, starting with the girl on the left. One, two, three, etc. . . .

Now try to count from one to twenty without taking into account your position in the circle. In other words, whoever wishes may begin. But the condition is, one must get from one up to twenty without any two people ever speaking at the same time. Some of you will have to speak more than once.

One, two, three, four *four*

No. Two people spoke at the same time, so we must go back to the beginning again. We'll start as many times as it takes, and even if we've reached nineteen and two voices come in on twenty, we'll have to go back to scratch. But we make it a point of honour not to give in.

Note carefully what is involved. On the one hand, there is absolute freedom. Each says a number when he chooses. On the other hand, there are two conditions which impose a great discipline: one is preserving the ascending order of the numbers, and the other is not speaking at the same time as someone else. This asks for a far greater concentration than at the start, when all you had to do was give your number in the order in which you were placed. This is another simple illustration of the relationship between concentration, attentiveness, listening and individual freedom. It also shows what a natural, living tempo involves, as the pauses are never artificial, no two pauses are alike and they are all filled with the thinking and concentration that bridges the silence.

I am very fond of this exercise, partly because of the way I came across it. One day in a bar in London an American director said to me, "My actors always do your 'great exercise'." I was puzzled. "What do you mean?" I asked. "The special exercise you do every day." I asked him what he was talking about, and he then described to me what we have just done. I had never heard of it and to this day I have no idea where it comes from. But I was happy to adopt it—since then we do it regularly and regard it as our own. It can easily last for twenty minutes or half an hour, in which case the tension gets very high, and the quality of listening in the group is transformed. I'm showing you this as an example of what one could call exercises of preparation.

Let us take another very different example to illustrate the same principle. Make a movement with your right arm, allow it to go anywhere, really anywhere, without thinking. When I give the signal, let it go, then stop the movement. Go!

Now hold the gesture just where it is, don't change or improve it, only try to feel what it is that you are expressing. Recognise that some sort of impression cannot fail to emanate from the attitude of your body. I look at all of you, and although you did not attempt to "tell" anything, to try to "say" anything, you just let your arm go where it wished, yet each of you is expressing something. Nothing is neutral. Let's do the experiment a second time: don't forget, it's a movement of the arm without premeditation.

Now hold the attitude just where it happens to be and try, without modifying your position, to feel a relationship between the hand, the arm, the shoulder, up to the muscles of the eye. Feel that it all has a meaning. Now allow the gesture to develop, to become more complete through a minimal movement, just a small adjustment.

Feel that in this minute change, something has transformed itself in the totality of your body, and the complete attitude becomes more unified and expressive.

We can't fail to realise how much we are continually expressing a thousand things with all the parts of our body. Most of the time this happens without our knowing it, and in an actor this makes for a diffuse attitude that cannot magnetise an audience.

Let us now try another experiment. Again it will be raising an arm in a simple gesture, but the difference is fundamental. Instead of making a movement that is your own, take a movement that I give you: place your hand, open, in front of you, the palm facing the outside. You do this not because you feel you want to, but because I'm asking you to, and you are prepared to go along with me without yet knowing where this will lead.

So welcome to the opposite of improvisation: earlier you made a gesture of your own choice, now you are doing one that is imposed. Accept doing this gesture without asking yourselves "What does it mean?" in an intellectual and analytical manner, otherwise you will remain on the "outside". Try to feel what it provokes in you. Something is given to you from the exterior, which is different from the free movement you made previously, and yet if you assume it totally, it is the same thing, it has become yours and you have become its. If you can experience this, it will throw light on the whole question of texts, of authorship, of direction. The true actor recognises that real freedom occurs at the moment when what comes from the outside and what is brought from within make a perfect blending.

Raise your hand once again. Try to feel how this movement is linked to the expression of the eyes. Don't try to be comic. Don't scowl in order to give the eyes and the face something to do, just let your sensitivity guide your tiniest muscles.

Now in the same way you listen to music, listen to how the feeling of the movement changes if you slowly rotate your hand, if you pass from this first position, with the palm on the outside, to this other position, with the palm facing the ceiling. What we are trying to do is feel not just the two attitudes but how in the passage from one to another a meaning is transformed. A meaning all the more meaningful because it is non-verbal and non-intellectual.

Next try to find personal variations within this movement: palm up, palm down. Articulate the gesture as you wish to, look for your own tempo. To find a living quality, one must be sensitive to the echo, the resonance produced by the movement in the rest of the body.

What we have just done comes under the general heading of "improvisation". There are thus two forms of improvisation, those which start from a total freedom of the actor, and those that take into account given, sometimes even constricting elements. In this case, and at each performance, the actor will have to "improvise", through a renewed, sensitive re-listening to the inner echoes of each detail in himself and in the others. If he does this, he will see that in its fine detail no performance can ever be exactly like another, and it is this awareness that gives him a constant renewal.

The experiments that we just crowded into a few minutes may normally take weeks and months. All through rehearsals and before each performance, an exercise or an improvisation can help to re-open each person to himself and a group to one another. Enjoyment is a great source of energy. An amateur has an advantage over a professional. As he works occasionally and entirely for pleasure, even if he doesn't have talent, he has enthusiasm. The professional needs re-invigorating if he is to avoid the stultifying efficiency of professionalism.

Another aspect of the difference between an amateur and a professional can be seen in the cinema. Amateur actors—sometimes a child, or someone found on the street—frequently play as well as professional actors. If, however, one says that all the parts in all films could be held equally by amateurs or professionals, this would be untrue. Where is the difference? If you ask an amateur to do in front of the camera the same actions he does in his daily life, he will in most cases do very well. This goes for most activities, from pottery to picking pockets.

An extreme example was in *The Battle of Algiers*, where the Algerians, who had lived through battles and had been in hiding in the resistance, were able to play, a few years later, the same gestures, which in turn evoked the same emotions. But normally if one asks someone who isn't a professional not only to reproduce movements which are deeply imprinted in his body, but also to conjure up for himself an emotional state, the amateur will almost invariably be completely lost. The professional actor's unique ability is to bring about in himself emotional states which belong not to him but to his character, without any visible contrivance or artificiality. This is very rare. Usually one can sense the gap between the actor himself and the state he is fabricating with varying degrees of skill. In the hands of a true artist, everything can seem natural, even if its outward form is so artificial that it has no equivalent in nature.

If one assumes that gestures from everyday life are automatically more "real" than those used in opera or in a ballet, one is mistaken. One need only look at the work coming out of the old Actors Studio—or perhaps from a distorted Actors Studio style—to understand that super-naturalism or hyper-realism are conventions that can seem just as artificial as singing in grand opera. Every single style or convention is artificial, with no preferences. Every style can appear phony. The job of the performer is to make any style natural. One comes back to the principle: I am given a word or gesture, and in the way I assume it, I make it "natural". But what, then, does "natural" mean? Natural means that the moment something happens there is no analysis, no comment, it just rings true.

Once I saw on television an extract of a film in which Jean Renoir said to an actress: "I learned from Michel Simon what was also the method of Louis Jouvet and certainly that of Moliere and Shakespeare: to understand one's character one must have no preconceived ideas. To do so, you should repeat the text over and over again, in a completely neutral manner, until it enters into you, until the understanding becomes personal and organic."

The suggestion of Jean Renoir is excellent, but like all suggestions, it is inevitably incomplete. I heard of a great director of Chekhov who rehearsed the plays for weeks in whispers. He had the text read very softly, preventing the actors from playing and thus polluting the words with immature or illegitimate impulses, such as showing, expressing, illustrating—or even enjoying the act of rehearsing. He asked them to murmur for weeks until the role installed itself deeply inside the actor. For Chekhov, it apparently brought good results, but I would find it very dangerous, unless within each day there were moments when this fine secrecy would be balanced by high-energy outgoing exercises and improvisations.

I met an American company touring a play of Shakespeare whose actors proudly told me about their method of work: on tour in Yugoslavia, each night they wandered through the streets of the town shouting out one chosen line from their role—for instance, "To be or not to be"—without allowing themselves to think of anything at all! They too ended up by being impregnated with their text, but I saw the performance and what a mindless mess this created! Obviously we are speaking here of a technique pushed to the point of absurdity.

In fact, one must combine the two approaches. It is very important in examining a scene for the first time to get a taste of it directly, by standing up and acting, like in an improvisation, without knowing what one is going to find. Discovering the text in a dynamic and active fashion is a rich way of exploring it and can give new depths to the intellectual examination, which is also necessary. But I shudder with horror at the Middle European technique which consists of sitting for weeks around a table to clarify the meanings of a text before allowing oneself to feel it in the body. This theory implies that before having established a kind of intellectual sketch, one is not allowed to stand up, as if one would not know what direction to take. This principle is, without doubt, very adapted to a military operation, for a good general undoubtedly brings his allies around a table before sending the tanks into enemy country, but the theatre is something else . . .

Let us go back for a moment to the differences between the amateur and the professional. When it concerns singing, dancing or acrobatics, the difference is visible because the techniques are very obvious. In singing, the note is either correct or not, the dancer wobbles or doesn't, the acrobat balances or falls. For the work of an actor, the demands are as great but it is nearly impossible to define the elements that are involved. One can see at once what is "not right", but what is needed for it to be right is so subtle and complex that it is very difficult to explain. For that reason, when one tries to find the truth of a relationship between two characters, the analytical, military method does not work. It cannot reach what is behind concepts and beyond definitions in the immense part of human experience that is hidden in the shadows.

Personally, I like to link within the same day different but complementary tasks: preparatory exercises that one must do regularly in the same way that one weeds and waters a garden; then practical work on the play, without preconceptions, by throwing oneself in at the deep end and experimenting; finally, a third phase, one of rational analysis, which can bring about a clarification of what one has just done.

This clarification is important only if it is inseparable from an intuitive understanding. Working around a table gives to analysis, a mental act, a much greater importance than one gives to the tool of intuition. This tool is more subtle and goes much further than analysis. Of course, intuition alone can also be very dangerous. As soon as one approaches the difficult problem inherent in a play, one finds oneself confronted by the necessity of intuition and the necessity of thought. Both are needed.

We discussed earlier the experiments that consisted in communicating the greatest possible emotion with the minimum amount of means. It is very interesting to see how the slightest expression, be it a word or a gesture, may be empty or full. One can say "Good day" to somebody without feeling either "good" or "day", and without even feeling the person one is speaking to. One may shake hands in an automatic manner—or else the same greeting can be illuminated with sincerity.

We have had great discussions with anthropologists about this theme during our travels. For them the difference between the European movement of shaking a hand and that of greeting both palms joined in the Indian manner, or hand on the heart in the Islamic way, is a cultural one. From the point of view of the actor, this theory has absolutely no relevance. We know it is possible to be just as hypocritical or just as true with the one gesture as with the other. We can inform a gesture with quality and meaning even if it doesn't belong to our culture. The actor must know that whatever movement he executes, it can either remain an empty shell or he can consciously fill it with a true significance. It's up to him.

Quality is found in detail. The presence of an actor, what it is that gives quality to his listening and his looking, is something rather mysterious, but not entirely so. It is not totally beyond his conscious and voluntary capacities. He can find this presence in a certain silence within himself. What one could call "sacred theatre", the theatre in which the invisible appears, takes root in this silence, from which all sorts of known and unknown gestures can arise. Through the degree of sensitivity in the movement, an Eskimo will be able to tell at once whether an Indian or African gesture is one of welcome or aggressivity. Whatever the code, a meaning can fill the form and understanding will be immediate. Theatre is always both a search for meaning and a way of making this meaning meaningful for others. This is the mystery.

A recognition of mystery is very important. When man loses his sense of awe, life loses its meaning and it is not for nothing that in its origins the theatre was a "mystery". However, the craft of the theatre cannot remain mysterious. If the hand that wields the hammer is imprecise in its movement, it will hit the thumb and not the nail. The ancient function of theatre must always be respected, but without the sort of respect that sends one to sleep. There is always a ladder to be climbed, leading from one level of quality to another. But where is this ladder to be found? Its rungs are details, the smallest of details, moment by moment. Details are the craft that leads to the heart of the mystery.

The Golden Fish

Each time I speak in public, it is an experiment in theatre. I try to draw the audience's attention to the fact that we are here and now in a theatrical situation. If you and I can observe in detail the process we are involved in at this very moment, then it will be possible for us to consider the meaning of theatre in a much less theoretical way. But today the experiment is much more complicated. For the very first time, instead of improvising, I have agreed to write a speech in advance, because the text is needed for publication. My aim is to make sure that this will not harm the process but rather help to make our joint experiment all the richer.

As I write these words, the author—"myself, number one"—is sitting in the south of France on a hot summer's day, trying to imagine the unknown: a Japanese audience in Kyoto—in what sort of hall, how many people, in what relationship I can't tell. And however carefully I choose my words, some of those listening will hear them through a translator in another language. Now, for you at this moment, "myself, number one", the author, has disappeared; he has been replaced by "myself, number two", the speaker. If the speaker reads these words, his head bent over his paper, delivering the contents in a monotonous, pedantic tone of voice, the very words that seem lively as I put them down on paper, will sink down into unbearable monotony, demonstrating once again what so often gives academic lectures a bad name. So "myself, number one" is like a playwright who has to have confidence that "myself, number two" will bring a new energy and a new detail into the text and the event. For those who understand English, it is the changes in the sound of the voice, the sudden changes of pitch, the crescendos, the fortissimos, the piano-pianos, the pauses, the silence—the immediate vocal music that carries with it the human dimension that can make you wish to listen, and this human dimension is just what we, and our computers, least understand in a precise, scientific way. It is feeling, feeling leading to passion, passion carrying conviction, conviction being the only spiritual instrument that makes one man concerned with another.

Even those of you who hear this at this moment through a translator are not isolated from a certain energy that begins gradually to link our attentions, for this energy reaches out into the room through sound and also through gesture; every movement the speaker makes, with the hand, with the body, whether conscious or unconscious, is a form of transmission—like an actor, I have to be aware of this, it's my responsibility—and you too play an active part, for within your silence is hidden an intensifier that sends your own private emotion back across our space, subtly encouraging me, amending my way of speech.

What has all this to do with theatre? Everything.

Let us together be very clear about our starting point. *Theatre* as a word is so vague that it is either meaningless or creates confusion because one person speaks about one aspect and another about something quite different. It is like speaking about life. The word is too big to carry meaning. Theatre is not to do with buildings, nor with texts, actors, styles or forms. The essence of theatre is within a mystery called "the present moment".

"The present moment" is astonishing. Like the fragment broken off a hologram, its transparency is deceptive. When this atom of time is split open, the whole of the universe is contained within its infinite smallness. Here, at this moment, on the surface, nothing in particular is happening, I am speaking, you are listening. But is this surface image a true reflection of our present reality? Of course not. None of us has suddenly shaken off his entire living fabric: even if they are momentarily dormant, our preoccupations, our relationships, our minor comedies, our deep tragedies are all present, like actors waiting in the wings. Not only are the casts of our personal dramas here, but like the chorus in an opera, crowds of minor characters are also lined up ready to enter, linking our private story with the outside world, with society as a whole. And within us at every moment, like a giant musical instrument ready to be played, are strings whose tones and harmonies are our capacity to respond to vibrations from the invisible spiritual world which we often ignore, yet which we contact with every new breath.

Were it possible suddenly to release into the open, into the arena of this hall, all our hidden imageries and motions, it would resemble a nuclear explosion, and the chaotic whirlpool of impressions would be too powerful for any of us to absorb. So we can see why an act of theatre in the present which releases the hidden collective potential of thought, image, feeling, myth and trauma is so powerful, and can be so dangerous.

Political oppression has always paid theatre its greatest compliment. In countries under the rule of fear, the theatre is the form which dictators watch closely and dread the most. For this reason, the greater our freedom, the more we ourselves must understand and discipline every act of theatre: to have meaning, it must obey very precise rules.

First of all, the chaos that could come from each individual releasing his own secret world must be unified into a shared experience. In other words, the aspect of reality that the performer is evoking must call up a response within the same area in each spectator so that for an instant the audience lives one collective impression. Thus, the basic material presented, the story or the theme, is, above all, there to provide a common ground, the potential field in which each member of the audience, whatever his age or his background, can find himself united with his neighbour in a shared experience.

Of course, it is very easy to find a common ground that is merely trivial, superficial, and therefore of no great interest. Obviously, the basis that links everyone together must be interesting. But what in fact does *in-*

teresting really mean? There is a test. In the millisecond-long instant when actor and audience interrelate, as in a physical embrace, it is the density, the thickness, the multi-layeredness, the richness—in other words, the quality of the moment that counts. Thus, any single moment can be thin, without great interest—or, on the contrary, deep in quality. Let me stress that this level of quality within the instant is the unique reference by which an act of theatre can be judged.

Now we must study more closely what we mean by a moment. Certainly if we could penetrate to the very core of a moment, we would find that there is no motion, each moment is the whole of all possible moments, and what we call time will have disappeared. But as we proceed outwards into the areas in which we normally exist, we see that each moment in time is related to the moment before and the moment following, in an ever-unfolding chain. So in a theatrical performance we are in the presence of an ineluctable law. A performance is a flow, which has a rising and falling curve. To reach a moment of deep meaning, we need a chain of moments which start on a simple, natural level, lead us towards intensity, then carry us away again. Time, which is so often an enemy in life, can also become our ally if we see how a pale moment can lead to a glowing moment, and then in turn to a moment of perfect transparency, before dropping again to a moment of everyday simplicity.

We can follow this better if we think of a fisherman making a net. As he works, care and meaning are present in every flick of the finger. He draws his thread, he ties the knots, enclosing emptiness with forms whose exact shapes correspond to exact functions. Then the net is thrown into the water, it is dragged to and fro, with the tide, against the tide, in many complex patterns. A fish is caught, an inedible fish, or a common fish good for stewing, maybe a fish of many colours, or a rare fish, or a poisonous fish, or at moments of grace a golden fish.

There is, however, a subtle distinction between theatre and fishing that must be underlined. In the case of the well-made net, it is the fisherman's luck whether a good or a bad fish is caught. In the theatre, those who tie the knots are also responsible for the quality of the moment that is ultimately caught in their net. It is amazing—the "fisherman" by his action of tying the knots influences the quality of the fish that land in his net!

The first step is all-important, and it is far more difficult than it seems. Surprisingly, this preliminary step is not given the respect it deserves. An audience may sit waiting for a performance to begin, wanting to be interested, hoping to be interested, persuading itself that it ought to be interested. It will only be irresistibly interested if the very first words, sounds or actions of the performance release deep within each spectator a first murmur related to the hidden themes that gradually appear. This cannot be an intellectual, least of all a rational, process. The theatre is in no way a discussion between cultivated people. The theatre, through the energy of sound, word, colour and movement, touches an emotional button that in turn sends tremors through the intellect. Once the performer is linked with the audience, the event can go in many ways. There are theatres that aim simply at producing a good ordinary fish that can be eaten without indigestion. There are pornographic theatres that aim wilfully at serving fish whose guts are clogged with poison. But let's assume we have the highest ambition, we only wish in performance to try to catch the golden fish.

Where does the golden fish come from? We don't know. From somewhere, we guess, in that collective, mythic unconscious, that vast ocean whose limits have never been discovered, whose depths have never been sufficiently explored. And where are we, the ordinary people in the audience? We are where we are as we enter the theatre, in ourselves, in our ordinary lives. Thus, the making of the net is the building of a bridge between ourselves as we usually are, in our normal condition, carrying our everyday world with us, and an invisible world that can reveal itself to us only when the normal inadequacy of perception is replaced by an infinitely more acute quality of awareness. But is this net made of holes or of knots? This question is like a koan, and to make theatre we must live with it all the time.

Nothing in theatre history so fully expresses this paradox as the structures we find in Shakespeare. In essence, his theatre is religious, it brings the invisible spiritual world into the concrete world of recognisable and visible shapes and actions. Shakespeare makes no concessions at either end of the human scale. His theatre does not vulgarise the spiritual to make it easier for the common man to assimilate, nor does it reject the dirt, the ugliness, the violence, the absurdity and the laughter of base existence. It slides effortlessly between the two, moment by moment, while in its grand forward thrust it intensifies the developing experience until all resistance explodes and the audience is awakened to an instant of deep insight into the fabric of reality. This moment cannot last. Truth can never be defined, nor grasped, but the theatre is a machine which enables all its participants to taste an aspect of truth within a moment; theatre is a machine for climbing and descending the scales of meaning.

Now we face the real difficulty. Catching a moment of truth demands that all the finest efforts of the actor, director, author and designer be united; no one can do it alone. Within one performance, there cannot be different aesthetics, conflicting aims. All techniques of art and craft have to serve what the English poet Ted Hughes calls a "negotiation" between our ordinary level and the hidden level of myth. This negotiation takes the form of bringing what is changeless together with the ever-changing everyday world, which is precisely where each performance is taking place. We are in contact with this world every second of our waking life, when the information recorded in our brain cells in the past is reactivated in the present. The other world which is permanently there is invisible, because our senses have no access to it, although it can be apprehended in many ways and at many times through our intuitions. All spiritual practises bring us towards the invisible world by helping us to withdraw from the world of impressions into stillness and silence. However, theatre is not the same as a spiritual discipline. Theatre is an external ally of the spiritual way, and it exists to offer glimpses, inevitably of short duration, of an invisible world that interpenetrates the daily world and is normally ignored by our senses.

The invisible world has no form, it does not change, or at least not in our terms. The visible world is always in movement, its characteristic is flux. Its forms live and die. The most complex form, the human being, lives and dies, cells live and die—and in exactly the same way, languages, patterns, attitudes, ideas, structures are born, decline and disappear. At certain rare moments in human history, it has been possible for artists to effect marriages so true between the visible and the invisible that their forms, be they temples, sculptures, paintings, stories or music seem to survive eternally, though even here we must be prudent and recognise that even eternity dies. It does not last forever.

A practical worker in the theatre, wherever he is in the world, has every reason to approach great traditional forms, especially those belonging to the East, with the humility and respect they deserve. They can carry him far beyond himself—way beyond the inadequate capacity for understanding and creativity that the twentieth-century artist must recognise as his true condition. A great ritual, a fundamental myth is a door, a door that is not there to be observed, but to be experienced, and he who can experience the door within himself passes through it most intensely. So the past is not to be arrogantly ignored. But we must not cheat. If we steal its rituals and its symbols and try to exploit them for our own purposes, we must not be surprised if they lose their virtue and become no more than glittering and empty decorations. We are constantly challenged to discriminate. In some cases, a traditional form is still living; in another, tradition is the dead hand that strangles the vital experience. The problem is to refuse the "accepted way", without looking for change for the sake of changing.

The central question, then, is one of form, the precise form, the apt form. We cannot do without it, life cannot do without it. But what does form mean? However often I return to this question, I am inevitably led to *sphota*, a word from classical Indian philosophy whose meaning is in its sound—a ripple that suddenly appears on the surface of still waters, a cloud that emerges from a clear sky. A form is the virtual becoming manifest, the spirit taking body, the first sound, the big bang.

In India, in Africa, in the Middle East, in Japan,

artists who work in the theatre are asking the same question: What is our form today? Where must we look to find it? The situation is confused, the question is confused, the answers are confused. They tend to fall into two categories. On the one hand, there is the belief that the great cultural powerhouses of the West—London, Paris and New York—have solved the problem, and all that is needed is to use their form, in the way that underdeveloped countries acquire industrial processes and technologies. The other attitude is the reverse. Artists in Third World countries often feel they have lost their roots, that they are caught up in the great wave coming from the West with all its twentieth-century imagery, so that they feel a need to refuse to imitate foreign models. This leads to a defiant return to cultural roots and ancient traditions. We see that this is a reflection of the two great contradictory thrusts of our time, outwards towards unity, inwards towards fragmentation.

Neither method produces good results, however. In many Third World countries, theatre groups tackle plays by European authors, such as Brecht or Sartre. Often they fail to recognise that these authors worked through a complex system of communication that belonged to their own time and place. In a completely different context, the resonance is no longer there. Imitations of the avant-garde experimental theatre of the sixties encounter the same difficulty. So sincere theatre workers in Third World countries, in a state of pride and despair, dig into their past and attempt to modernise their myths, rituals and folklore, but unfortunately this often results in a poor mixture that is "neither fish nor fowl".

How then can one be true to the present? Recently, I made journeys that took me to Portugal, Czechoslovakia and Romania. In Portugal, the poorest of the West European countries, I was told "people don't go to the theatre or to the cinema anymore." "Ah," I said understandingly, "with all your economic difficulties, people haven't the money." "Not at all!" was the surprising answer. "It is just the opposite. The economy is slowly improving. Before, when money was scarce, life was very grey, and an outing, whether to the theatre or the cinema was a necessity, so of course one saved up for it. Today, people are beginning to have a little more to spend, and the entire range of twentieth-century consumer possibilities is within their grasp. There is video, video-cassettes, compact discs, and to satisfy the eternal need to be with other people there are restaurants, charter flights, package tours. Then clothes, shoes, haircuts . . .

Cinema and theatre are still there, but they have sunk very low in the order of priorities."

From the market-orientated West, I proceeded to Prague and Bucharest. Here again, as indeed in Poland, in Russia, in almost all the ex-Communist countries, there is the same cry of despair. A few years ago, people fought to have seats in the theatres: now they play often to no more than 25 percent of their capacity. Again, in a totally different social context, one is faced with the same phenomenon of a theatre that no longer appeals.

In the days of totalitarian oppression, a theatre was one of the rare places where for a short period one could feel free, one could either escape into a more romantic, more poetic existence, or else, hidden and protected by the anonymity of an audience, one could join by laughter or applause in acts of defiance of the authority. Line after line of a respectable classic could give the actor, by the slightest stress on a word or an imperceptible gesture, the opportunity to enter into a secret complicity with the spectator, thus expressing what otherwise was too dangerous to express. Now that need is gone and the theatre is forced to confront an unpalatable fact—that the gloriously full houses of the past were packed for many valid reasons but that they were not concerned with a true theatre experience of the play itself.

Let us look again at the situation in Europe. From Germany all the way to the East, including the vast Russian continent, and also westwards through Italy to Portugal and Spain, there has been a long series of totalitarian governments. The characteristic of all forms of dictatorship is that culture is frozen. No matter what the forms, they no longer have the possibility to live, die, replace one another according to natural laws. A certain range of cultural forms is recognised as safe and respectable and is institutionalised, whereas all other forms are considered suspect and are either driven underground or completely stamped out. The period of the twenties and the thirties was for the European theatre a time of extraordinary animation and fertility. The major technical innovations—revolving stages, open stages, lighting effects, projections, abstract scenery, functional constructions—were all achieved during this period. Certain styles of acting, certain relations with audiences, certain hierarchies, such as the place of the director, or the importance of the designer, became established. They were in tune with their times. There followed enormous social upheavals; war, massacre, revolution and counterrevolution, disillusion, rejection of old ideas, hunger for new stimuli, a hypnotic attraction to all that was new and different. Today the lid has been lifted. But the theatre, rigidly confident in its old structures, has not changed. It is no longer part of its time. As a result, for so many reasons, all through the world the theatre is in crisis. This is good, this is necessary.

It is of vital importance to make a clear distinction. "Theatre" is one thing, whereas "the theatres" is something quite different. "The theatres" are the boxes; a box is not its content, any more than an envelope is a letter. We choose our envelopes according to the size and length of our communication. Sadly, the parallel falters at this point: it is easy to throw an envelope into the fire; it is far more difficult to throw away a building, especially a beautiful building, even when we feel instinctively that it has outlived its purpose. It is harder still to discard the cultural habits printed in our minds, habits of aesthetics, artistic practices and traditions. Yet "theatre" is a fundamental human need, while "theatres" and their forms and styles are only temporary and replaceable boxes.

So we return to the problems of the empty theatres and we see that the question cannot be one of reform— a word which in English quite precisely means remaking the old forms. As long as the attention is locked onto form, the answer will be purely formal—and disappointing in practise. If I am talking so much about forms, it is to stress that a quest for new forms cannot in itself be an answer. The problem for countries with traditional theatre styles is the same. If modernising means putting the old wine in new bottles, the formal trap is still tightly closed. If the attempt for the director, the designer, the actor is to take naturalistic reproductions of present-day images as a form, again he finds, to his disappointment, that he can hardly go farther than what television presents hour after hour.

A theatre experience which lives in the present must be close to the pulse of the time, just as a great fashion designer is never blindly looking for originality but is mysteriously blending his creativity with the ever-changing surface of life. Theatre art must have an everyday facet—stories, situations, themes must be recognisable, for a human being is, above all, interested in the life he knows. Theatre art must also have a substance and a meaning. This substance is the density of the human experience; every artist longs to capture this in his work in one way or another, and perhaps he senses that meaning arises through the possibility of contacting the invisible source beyond his normal limitations which gives meaning to meaning. Art is a spinning wheel, rotating around a still centre which we can neither grasp nor define.

So what is our aim? It is a meeting with the fabric of life, no more and no less. Theatre can reflect every aspect of human existence, so every living form is valid, every form can have a potential place in dramatic expression. Forms are like words; they only take on meaning when used rightly. Shakespeare had the largest vocabulary of any English poet, constantly adding to the words at his disposal, combining obscure philosophical terms with the crudest of obscenities, until eventually there were over 25,000 at his fingertips. In the theatre, there are infinitely more languages, beyond words, through which communication is established and maintained with the audience. There is body language, sound language, rhythm language, colour language, costume language, scenery language, lighting language—all to be added to those 25,000 available words. Every element of life is like a word in a universal vocabulary. Images from the past, images from tradition, images from today, rockets to the moon, revolvers, coarse slang, a pile of bricks, a flame, a hand on the heart, a cry from the guts, the infinite musical shades of the voice—these are like nouns and adjectives with which we can make new phrases. Can we use them well? Are they necessary, are they the means that make what they express more vivid, more poignant, more dynamic, more refined and more true?

Today, the world offers us new possibilities. This great human vocabulary can be fed by elements that in the past have never come together. Each race, each culture can bring its own word to a phrase which unites mankind. Nothing is more vital to the theatre culture of the world than the working together of artists from different races and backgrounds.

When separate traditions come together, at first there are barriers. When, through intense work, a common aim is discovered, the barriers vanish. The moment when the barriers vanish, the gestures and the tones of voice of one and all become part of the same language, expressing for a moment one shared truth in which the audience is included: this is the moment to which all theatre leads. These forms can be old or new, they can be ordinary or exotic, elaborate or simple, sophisticated or naïve. They can come from the most unexpected sources, they can appear to be totally contradictory, even to the point of seeming mutually exclusive. In fact, if in the place of unity of style, they scrape and jangle against one another, this can be healthy and revealing.

The theatre must not be dull. It must not be conventional. It must be unexpected. Theatre leads us to truth through surprise, through excitement, through games, through joy. It makes the past and the future part of the present, it gives us a distance from what normally envelops us and abolishes the distance between us and what is normally far away. A story from today's newspapers can suddenly seem much less true, less intimate than something from another time, another land. It is the truth of the present moment that counts, the absolute sense of conviction that can only appear when a unity binds performer and audience. This appears when the temporary forms have served their purpose and have brought us into this single, unrepeatable instant when a door opens and our vision is transformed.

There Are No Secrets

There is a moment when one cannot go on saying no. All through the years, when people ask me, "Can we come and watch one of your rehearsals?" I answer "No." I am compelled to do so, because of certain bad experiences.

At the very beginning I did let visitors into rehearsals. I allowed a quiet and modest student to sit discreetly at the back of the auditorium during rehearsals of a Shakespeare play. He was no problem, I was hardly aware of his existence, until the day I found him in the bar of the local pub, explaining to the actors how they should play their scenes. Despite this experience, a few years later I allowed a very serious author to observe the process, as he had convinced me it was important for his own research. My only condition was that he should publish nothing about what he witnessed. In spite of his promise, a book appeared, full of inaccurate impressions, and betraying the essential bond of trust which is the basis for the actor and director's capacity to work together. Later, when I was putting on a play for the first time in France, I discovered that it was quite normal for the owner of the theatre to come into the stalls with her rich friends, in fur coats and jewels, chattering excitedly, watching these strange and funny creatures called actors at work, and not hesitating to make loud and often humorous comments about what they saw.

"Never again!" I swore. And as the years go by, I see more and more how important it is for actors, who are by nature fearful and oversensitive, to know that they are totally protected by silence, intimacy and secrecy. When you have this security, then day after day you can experiment, make mistakes, be foolish, certain in the knowledge that no one outside the four walls will ever know, and from that point you begin to find the strength that helps you to open up, both to yourself and to the others. I have found that the presence of even one person somewhere in the dark behind me is a continual distraction and source of tension. An onlooker can even tempt a director to show off, to intervene when he should have remained silent, for fear of disappointing the visitor by seeming ineffective.

This is why I have always said no to the constant requests to observe our work. Yet I understand how strongly people want to know what goes on, what we really do. So today in this workshop, I feel like saying "Yes, there are no secrets." I will try to describe, fact by fact, the working process, and to make it very precise I will use my recent production in Paris of *The Tempest* as an example.

First of all, the choice of the play. We are an international group, and most of us have worked together for a long time. We had finished the long cycle of work over many years with the *Mahabharata* in French, the *Mahabharata* in English and the *Mahabharata* on film. We had then put together a season of South African plays and music in our theatre in Paris, in honor of both the bicentenary of the French Revolution and of the Year of Human Rights. I now felt the need, for the group of actors and myself, to take a completely new direction and to leave behind all the imagery from the past that had become so much part of our lives. I had become interested in the strange and elusive relationship between the brain and the mind, and upon reading a book by a doctor, Oliver Sacks, called *The Man Who Mistook His Wife for a Hat*, I began to see a possibility of dramatising this mystery through the behavioural patterns of certain neurological cases. Our group was very interested in the new field of work that this proposed.

However, when one works from a theme that has no apparent form or structure, it is essential to give oneself unlimited time. The advantage of an existing play is that the author has already completed all his work, so it is possible to determine how long the staging needs to take and thus fix a date for the first performance. In fact, this is the only difference between an experimental project and putting on an existing play. Both actions need to be equally experimental, only the time that is needed differs: in one case, a programme for a theatre can be announced, in the other case, dates must be left open.

Finding, therefore, that we needed time for our neurological studies and research to develop, and yet recognising the practical responsibility of having to maintain a theatre and an organisation, I looked around for a play that would suit our international group, that would have a quality that could inspire the actors and simultaneously bring something of value to the audience, something related to the needs and realities of our era. Such reasoning has always led me straight to Shakespeare. Shakespeare is always the model that no one has surpassed, his work is always relevant and always contemporary.

The Tempest is a play I know well, as I had first directed it some thirty-five years ago at Stratford with the great English actor John Gielgud as Prospero. I had returned to it a few years later in the same theatre as an experiment, in collaboration with another English director. When, in Paris in 1968, I did the first workshop with actors from many cultures that was eventually to lead to the creation of our International Centre, I chose scenes from *The Tempest* as the raw material out of which to develop our improvisations and research. So the play has always been very present in my spirit. But, curiously, I never thought of *The Tempest* as being the answer to my current problem until one day, while sitting in a garden in London and speaking about my dilemma in searching for the right subject for our group of actors, a friend suggested *The Tempest*. Immediately, I saw that this was exactly what we needed and that it was exactly right for our actors. Not for the first time in my life, I was aware that all the factors needed for a decision were already prepared in the unconscious part of the mind, without the conscious mind having any part in the deliberations. This is why it is hard to answer the first question that is often asked—"How do you choose a play?" Is it accident or choice? Is it frivolous or the result of deep thought? Rather, I think, we prepare ourselves by the options we reject until the true solution, which was already there, suddenly comes into the open. One lives within a pattern: to ignore this is to take many false directions, but the moment the hidden movement is respected, it becomes the guide, and in retrospect one can trace a clear pattern that continues to unfold.

The moment my conscious mind became aware that *The Tempest* might be the answer, the advantages it offered became clear. First of all, a play of Shakespeare's can only be undertaken when one is convinced that one has the right actors. It is foolish for a director to say, "I want to stage *Hamlet*," and then begin to wonder who can play the part. It is possible to carry in oneself for years the desire to work on a great text, but the practical decision can only come when one sees before one's eyes the indispensable partners, the interpreters of the major roles. *King Lear* was a subject that had haunted me for a very long time, but the moment for putting this phantom into a concrete form arose only when the unique actor in England capable of taking on this task was mature and ready—this was Paul Scofield. In the case of *The Tempest*, I realised that we had with us an African actor, Sotigui Kouyaté, who could bring something new, different and perhaps truer than any European actor to the major role of Prospero the magician, and that the other actors from non-English cultures could illuminate this elusive play through the light of their own traditions, which at times are closer to the spirituality of Elizabethan England than the urban values of contemporary Europe.

So the starting point was clear. We only needed a date. I calculated the rehearsal time we needed—fourteen weeks—but I had underestimated the time needed for preparation. A few weeks later I became alarmed, so I reshuffled all our plans and postponed the beginning of rehearsals by a couple of months.

Jean-Claude Carrière began work on a French translation and at the same time I started discussions on the visual aspects with the designer, Chloé Obolensky. Now this is the most delicate part of the process, as it contains its own contradiction. There has to be a space arranged in a suitable way, there have to be costumes, so it would seem obvious that this demands planning and organisation. However, experience shows again and again that decisions taken by a director and a designer before rehearsals start are invariably inferior to decisions taken much later in the process. By then, the director and designer are no longer alone with their personal vision and aesthetics, but are nourished by the infinitely deeper vision, both of the play and of its theatrical possibilities, that comes from the rich, interweaving explorations of a whole group of imaginative and creative individuals.

Before rehearsals, not only is the very best work of director and designer limited and subjective—worse, it imposes cast-iron forms, whether in stage action or in clothing on the actors, and can often crush or handicap a natural development. So the true working method involves a very subtle balancing act for which there are no rules and which changes each time, between what must be prepared in advance and what can safely be left open. At first, I looked back to my past productions and experiments with this play and I saw that there was nothing I wished to retain: they belonged to another world, another understanding. As I reread the play in this new context, certain flickering forms began to dance very obscurely in corners of my mind. My first production in Stratford had followed the accepted view that *The Tempest* is a spectacle and therefore had to be brought alive by elaborate stage effects. So I enjoyed myself, designing striking visual moments, composing atmospheric electronic music, introducing goddesses and dancing shepherds. Intuitively, I now felt that spectacle was not the answer, that it disguised the deepest qualities of the play and that whatever we did must take the form of a series of games—*playing* in its most literal sense—executed by a small group of players. Intellectually, I analysed this as meaning that as the play has no realistic roots, neither in geography, nor in history, and as the island is simply an image and a symbol, it cannot be evoked by any form of literal illustration. So in completing my first reading, I scribbled on the last blank page a sketch of a Zen garden, as in Kyoto, where an island is suggested by a rock and water by dry pebbles. This could be the formal space in which the actors, with no more than their own imaginations to help them, could directly suggest all the levels of the theme.

When Chloé Obolensky and I had our first discussion, we only saw the disadvantages of such a solution. Pebbles would be hard to walk on, they would make a continual, distracting noise and they would make sitting awkward and uncomfortable. So the Zen garden was discarded, but we remained convinced that the principle of suggestion by the lightest of means remained valid. The question before us now was whether to evoke nature with a natural surface, such as earth and sand, or to evoke it imaginatively on an acting surface, such as wood or carpet.

Every designer and every director of *The Tempest* is forced right at the opening to face a major difficulty. The play has a unity of place, the island, except for the first scene, which takes place on a ship at sea during a storm. Is it necessary to violate this unity by making a complicated realistic stage picture for the first moments of the play? The better this is done, the more it destroys the possibility of evoking the island subsequently in a non-naturalistic convention and the harder it makes the playing of the second long quiet scene of exposition, when Prospero tells his life to his daughter. If the convention chosen is one of elaborate pictorial scenery, the solution is easy: one makes an impressive shipwreck, then one slides into place a desert island. But if one rejects this approach, one must discover what can effortlessly convey at one moment sea and at the next, dry land. We agreed to leave this problem unsolved, to be clarified by what we would see once the actors began to work in our space.

Our group was mainly composed of actors who had already worked in the International Centre. The principle behind the casting was to re-interpret the play in the light of traditional cultures, so we had an African Prospero, an African Ariel, a Balinese spirit, and a young German actor joining us for the first time, to bring a new vision to the part of Caliban, so often presented either as a monster made up of rubber and plastic or as a Negro, exploiting the colour of his skin to illustrate in a very banal way the notion of a slave. I wanted Caliban presented in a fresh image, with the ferocious, dangerous, uncontrollable rebellion of an adolescent of today.

Miranda, as conceived by Shakespeare, is very young indeed, she is precisely fourteen years old, Ferdinand hardly older. It seemed obvious that these parts would yield their true beauty if they were played by actors of the right age, and especially if Miranda possessed the grace that a traditional upbringing could give. We found an Indian girl, trained as a dancer by her mother from an early age, and another very young girl, half Vietnamese.

The beginning of the process was to withdraw from our normal surroundings, so with all the cast, the assistants and Jean-Claude Carrière we set off for Avignon, where we had been lent accommodations and a large rehearsal space in the ancient cloisters of a former monastery. Here, in peace and absolute seclusion, we spent ten days in preparation. Everyone arrived with his copy of *The Tempest* in hand, but the scripts were never opened. We did not once touch the play. First we exercised our bodies, then our voices.

We did group exercises whose sole purpose was to develop a quick responsiveness, a hand, ear and eye contact, a shared awareness that is easily lost and has to be constantly renewed, to bring together the separate individuals and form them into a sensitive, vibrant team. The need and the rules are the same as in sport, only an acting team must go farther: not only the bodies, but the thoughts and the feelings must all come into play and stay in tune. This calls for vocal exercises and improvisations, both comic and serious. After a few days our study included words, single words, then clusters of words and eventually isolated phrases in English and French to try to make real for everyone including the translator the special nature of Shakespearean writing. In my experience, it is always a mistake for actors to begin their work with intellectual discussion, as the rational mind is not nearly as potent an instrument of discovery as the more secret faculties of intuition. The possibility of intuitive understanding through the body is stimulated and developed in many different ways. If this happens, within the same day there can be moments of repose when the mind can peacefully play its true role. Only then will analysis and discussion of the text find their natural place.

After this first period of quiet concentration, we returned to our theatre in Paris, the Bouffes du Nord. Chloé, the designer, had prepared for the first rehearsal not scenic elements but "possibilities". This meant ropes hanging from the ceiling, ladders, planks, blocks of wood, packing cases. Also carpets, piles of earth of different colors, spades and shovels—elements that are not

linked to any aesthetic conception but are just imple-
ments that the actors can grab, use and discard.

Each scene was improvised in countless ways, the actors being encouraged in complete freedom to use all that
the space and the multitude of objects suggested to their
imagination. As director, I would make suggestions, have
new ideas—often having to criticise my own proposals
and withdraw them after seeing them put into practise
by the actors. If an observer were admitted during this
period, he would form an impression of utter confusion,
of minds being made up and unmade in bewildering patterns. Even the actors lost their way, and the role of the
director is to keep track of what is being explored and
for what purpose. If he does so, this first explosion of
energy is not as chaotic as it seems, for it produces a
vast amount of raw material out of which the final shapes
can be drawn.

The task is helped by the challenge of the play itself.
The quality of the play, the enigma that it contains, makes
it a stern judge. The play is the rigour, the austerity that
helps to separate the valuable from the useless within
the mass of undeveloped ideas. In the case of *The Tempest*, the text is of such quality that every invention and
every decoration appears unnecessary and even vulgar.
One is rapidly caught in a frightening trap: anything that

one does after a first moment of enthusiasm is soon inadequate and beside the mark. The opposite, however,
is even worse, as one cannot escape by doing nothing;
no text can ever "speak for itself". The simple way is
always the hardest to find, for a mere lack of invention
is not simplicity, just dull theatre. So while one must
intervene, one must also remain harshly critical of one's
attempts at intervention.

So we invented, we tried, we explored, we discussed.
The first scene, the shipwreck, was approached in at least
twenty different ways. There were planks to suggest the
deck of a ship, carried by the actors who, squatting,
placed them across their knees to create the steep angles
of a tilting deck. Ariel and the spirits played many aesthetic games, tossing a model boat over the heads of the
actors, crushing the boat with a rock or drowning it in
a pail of water. Sailors climbed ladders, or scrambled to
the various balconies in the auditorium, the courtiers
sat in cramped cabins under swinging lanterns, while
spirits in masks playfully replaced the mutinous sailors.
Everything was exciting the moment we thought of it,
and unconvincing when looked at coolly the next day,
when it was invariably scrapped without regret. In despair, we abandoned all forms of illustration, placing the
actors in strict formations like in an oratorio, using their

voices to imitate the sounds of wind and waves—this seemed promising, until we looked at it again and found it formal and inhuman.

Nothing seemed appropriate. Each image had its drawbacks: too conventional, too farfetched, too intellectual, too déjà vu. One by one, all the gadgets were thrown out, the boards, the ropes, the steel ladders, the model ships. Yet nothing is ever lost completely—a trace would remain and return unexpectedly weeks later in a different scene. For instance, if we had not spent so much time experimenting with a model ship in the first scene, the idea would never have arisen for Ariel to play, in his first scene with Prospero, with a ship with a red sail balanced on his head, where it is genuinely useful, for it is just the element needed to give a colourful support to his actions. The ropes that seemed so heavy-handed in the ship scene became very valuable at one precise moment three scenes later, where a rope, used by Caliban who normally would never seem to need to climb into the air, was least expected. In the same way, had one of the musicians amongst his bag of "possibilities" not found a hollow tube full of pebbles that makes a swishing sound like the waves of the sea, we might never have discovered the one simple device that could replace all our first clumsy attempts to evoke the storm and suggest to the audience in the very first seconds that it is on the island of the imagination that the performance will take place.

The main work, day after day, was wrestling with the words and their meaning. Meaning also emerges from the text slowly, by trial and error. A text comes to life only through detail, and detail is the fruit of understanding. At first an actor can give no more than a broad, generalised impression of what a line contains and often he needs to be helped. This can be by advice and criticism. There is also a certain technique which we evolved with singers in *Carmen*. When the singer proved unable to break his generalised acting into meaningful and detailed actions, one of my collaborators, a very fine actor himself, would play the part for him. It might seem that we were following the ways of the worst old-fashioned productions, where the singer is required slavishly to copy what he is shown. However, this was not the aim. Once the imitation was successfully mastered, the old technique was broken and the singer was told to discard completely what he had learned. In every case, the singer, having tasted in himself what detailed acting means—something that could never be conveyed by description—could now proceed to discover his own details in his own way. This process also helped those of our actors who had never played Shakespeare before: by imitation they could get a direct "feel" of a scene by assuming a precise pattern created by a more experienced actor. Once it had served its purpose, it could be cast away, as a child throws aside a rubber life belt once he learns to swim. Similarly, it stimulates understanding when actors exchange roles in rehearsal and receive new impressions of the characters they are seeking to inhabit. What must be avoided is the director demonstrating the way he himself would like the part to be played and then forcing the actor to assume and stick to this alien, imposed construction. Instead, the actor must be stimulated all the time so that in the end he finds his own way.

Amongst many other difficulties in this play, the scenes with the shipwrecked court of nobles is particularly baffling. Shakespeare has written these scenes in a way that leaves the characters underdeveloped and their situation very little dramatised. It is as though in his last play he deliberately cast aside all the techniques he had evolved throughout his career for engaging an audience's interest and identification with his characters. As a result, these scenes can easily be colourless and dull: the more they are played for psychological realism, the more one discovers the thinness of the characterisation. It seemed clear to us that Shakespeare, in writing *The Tempest* as a fable wished to maintain a lightness of tone throughout, like an Oriental storyteller, avoiding the intense moments of serious drama that his tragedies contain. We tried to develop the incongruity of the situation of the nobles in a world of illusions through the constant presence of the spirits—misleading the humans, tricking them and inciting them to reveal their hidden intentions. This needed many improvisations and inventions created by the spirits themselves, and with their help we felt we were discovering how to evoke different images of the island with the lightest of means. Little did we know that this would be the source of our greatest crisis.

To explain this, I must return to the subject of the stage setting. Over the first weeks, watching the play come to life, the designer and I became more and more convinced that what we needed was an empty space, in which the imagination could have free play. We had rejected the ropes and the other gadgets of the early days, we also rejected wooden and carpeted floors, being convinced that the texture of the story demanded that it be played out amongst natural elements. So, during a weekend, Chloé brought several tons of red earth into the theatre. In order to give life and variety to the actors' movements, she carefully moulded the ground into little rises and hillocks, made a deep hole in one of the mounds, and the result was that the theatre was transformed into a glowingly impressive place of epic proportions.

However, as we began to rehearse, we discovered that the grandeur of the space made our actions seem pitifully inadequate. We had now reached the point where we were suggesting the ship with a few bamboo sticks held horizontally, and which later when held upright, were all that was required to evoke the forest. The spirits needed no more than a few palm leaves, blades of grass or twigs to play tricks with the imagination. But to our dismay we found that the new setting refused to collaborate in this work of suggestion. The area did not evoke an island in the mind; instead it became a real island, a tragic landscape that was waiting for a King Lear. So we restaged every scene to suit the scenery, to match its proportions, using long poles, infinitely larger objects and, for the ship at sea, we even considered covering the stage with smoke, as this real landscape could not merely by the power of acting be transformed into the sea. Then Chloé and I recognised to our shared alarm that we were falling back into the classic trap of having to adapt the acting to the set, and of attempting to justify the storm in *The Tempest* by placing one realistic image on top of another. We could see no way out. The stage picture and acting picture did not go together, and there was no apparent solution.

What saved us was an event which has become, for many years now, part of our rehearsal methods. At a certain point, roughly two-thirds of the way through rehearsals, when the actors know their lines, understand the story, have found essential links between the characters—and when a physical production is taking shape in terms of movements, objects, furniture, scenery, elements of costume—we abandon everything and go one afternoon to a school, where, in some tiny cramped basement surrounded by about a hundred schoolchildren, we improvise directly a version of the play using the possibilities of space in which we find ourselves, taking hold only of the objects lying around the room, using them freely for whatever we need.

The aim of the exercise is to be like good storytellers. Almost invariably, the children know nothing in advance about the play we bring them, so our job is to find the most immediate ways of capturing their imagination and never letting it go, making the story come alive freshly, moment by moment. This is always very revealing, and a couple of hours carries our work several weeks ahead: we can see clearly what is good, what is bad, what we have understood, where we have made false guesses, and so together we discover many essential truths about what a play needs. Children are far better and more precise than most friends and drama critics, they have no prejudices, no theories, no fixed ideas. They come wanting to be fully involved in what they experience, but if they are not interested, they have no reason to hide their lack of attention—we see it at once and can read it truly as a failure on our part.

On this occasion, working on a carpet in a very small space, the play came to life at once. As there was no attempt to state anything in a decorative way, the audience's imagination was free to respond to every suggestion. So the actors banged doors and shook thick plastic curtains to evoke the storm, piles of shoes became the logs that Ferdinand has to gather, Ariel dragged a wire net from the garden to imprison the nobles. And so on. The performance had no aesthetic style, it was rough, immediate and totally successful, because the means suited the aim, and in these conditions the story of the play was totally conveyed. It left the designer and me alert to many new questions—and very worried indeed.

One has seen very often how young groups playing in very small spaces can be very successful, while if their work is transferred to a larger stage, it can seem pitifully insufficient. Energy and quality often are inseparable from the context in which they occur. Because of this, we both recognised clearly that the amusing inventions that worked so vividly in a small room would seem childish and amateur if we quite literally reproduced them in the challenging space of our own theatre, which naturally demands a different quality of invention. At the same time, we had witnessed practical evidence of our own basic theory—that this play needs to be freed from any decorative statement that confines the imagination.

My own response was to say that we must revert to the idea of a carpet, as a neutral but attractive area on which anything can happen. Chloé disagreed—but we were both convinced that this proposition must be immediately put to the test. To our actors' astonishment, when they returned to the theatre, they found in the middle of the red earth our large Persian carpet, which was the area on which we had long ago played *The Conference of the Birds*. We did a run-through of the play at once, using all the elements with which we had rehearsed in the theatre, but confining the action to within the carpet. The results were oddly contradictory. On the one hand, the play gained enormously by having its acting space reduced. In becoming more concentrated, the fact that it no longer spread out to the walls of the theatre freed us from a certain naturalism: the carpet became a formal space, a space for acting, and suddenly the use of thin bamboo sticks and tiny objects made sense again. What had seemed ridiculous in the large space now recovered its natural meaning. On the other hand, as Chloé had feared, the designs of the Persian carpet, which had been so evocative for the Sufi poem of *The Conference of the Birds*, here were irritatingly distracting. Where we wanted the spectator to imagine sea, sand and sky, the intricate Oriental designs refused to co-operate, as their very beauty made other illusions impossible; it was as though they were speaking to the audience loudly in another language. In the school, of course, the carpet had been invisible, it was just the plain, familiar, worn-out classroom rug and so it had no existence.

We wondered whether we could use a simple carpet without a design on it, and in the same breath we recognised that this would be like wall-to-wall carpeting in an office or hotel, bringing with it irrelevant present-day associations. We tried sprinkling some sand onto the Persian carpet, but the result was lamentable. Luckily, we had a few days' holiday planned just at this moment. I spent them looking at the ground, comparing every sort of surface on building sites, parks and waste lands. When I returned, Chloé had framed our carpet with bamboo poles. Then she took up the carpet, but, like an imprint on the ground, its shape remained, a precise rectangle outlined in bamboo. This Chloé filled with sand. It was a carpet still, but a carpet made of sand. The actors rehearsed and we knew that our central problem had found its solution. Then to give the space one strong point of reference, Chloé placed two rocks in it. Eventually we took one away.

Afterwards, to our great satisfaction, certain critics called this a "playing field", after the term one uses in England exclusively for sports, or, as one describes the recreation yard in a school, a "playground", both of which terms cover exactly what we had first set out to achieve—a place for playing in, or, in other words, a place in which theatre does not pretend to be anything other than theatre. Then someone else wrote, "It's a Zen garden," and I remembered my very first starting point. As always, one has to go into a forest and back to find the plant that is growing besides one's own front door. Often I have found, long after a production is finished, a note or a little sketch discarded and completely forgotten, showing that somewhere in the subconscious lay the answer that one then had to go through months of searching to rediscover.

I describe this experience with one aspect of a production—the design—in detail, because it can be seen as a clear metaphor for every other aspect. It is the same process of trial and error, search, elaboration, rejection and chance that makes the actor's interpretation take form, that integrates the work of the musicians or the lighting designer into an organic whole.

I say "chance", and this could be misleading. Chance exists; it is not the same as luck, it obeys rules we cannot understand, but certainly it can be helped and favoured. There must be many efforts—all efforts create a field of energy, and this at a critical moment attracts towards it a solution. On the other hand, experimenting chaotically for its own sake can go on indefinitely without ever reaching a coherent conclusion. Chaos is only useful if it leads to order.

This is where the director's role becomes clear. The director must have from the start what I have called a "formless hunch", that is to say, a certain powerful yet shadowy intuition that indicates the basic shape, the source from which the play is calling to him. What he needs most to develop in his work is a sense of listening. Day after day, as he intervenes, makes mistakes or watches what is happening on the surface, inside he must be listening, listening to the secret movements of the hidden process. It is in the name of this listening that he will be constantly dissatisfied, will continue to accept and reject until suddenly his ear hears the secret sound it is expecting and his eye sees the inner form that has been waiting to appear. Yet on the surface all the steps must be concrete, rational. Questions of visibility, pace, clarity, articulation, energy, musicality, variety, rhythm— these all need to be observed in a strictly practical and professional way. The work is the work of an artisan, there is no place for false mystification, for spurious magical methods. The theatre is a craft. A director works and listens. He helps the actors to work and listen.

This is the guide. This is why a constantly changing process is not a process of confusion but one of growth. This is the key. This is the secret. As you see, there are no secrets.

Sources

"The Slyness of Boredom" is adapted from "Le Diable c'est l'Ennui", a transcript of a workshop given in Paris on the 9th & 10th of March 1991.

"The Golden Fish" & "There Are No Secrets" are adapted from speeches given in Kyoto on the occasion of the Inamori Foundation prizegiving in November 1991.

THE THEATRE OF THE ABSURD
by Martin Esslin

Within five years of its premier in 1953, Samuel Beckett's *Waiting for Godot* had been translated into more than twenty languages and seen by more than a million spectators. Its popularity marked the emergence of a new type of theatre whose proponents—Beckett, Ionesco, Genet, Pinter, and others—shattered dramatic conventions and paid scant attention to psychological realism. In 1961, Martin Esslin gave a name to this phenomenon in the authoritative, engaging, and readable study, *The Theatre of the Absurd*.

Drama/1-4000-7523-8

PLAYING SHAKESPEARE
An Actor's Guide
by John Barton

With the Royal Shakespeare Company actors, John Barton demonstrates how to adapt Elizabethan theater to the modern stage. The director explicates Shakespeare's verse and prose, speeches and soliloquies, and naturalistic and heightened language to discover the essence of the characters. They explore nuance in Shakespearean theater, such as evoking irony and ambiguity, and striking the delicate balance of passion and intellectual thought. A practical and essential guide, *Playing Shakespeare* will stand for years as the authoritative favorite among actors, scholars, teachers, and students.

Drama/0-385-72085-8

THE ACTOR'S AUDITION
by David Black

The audition is the first—and most essential—test of any actor's craft, one that is typically performed for a very tough audience. This practical, hands-on guide by a veteran producer covers every aspect of the auditioning process: the monologue, the cold reading, the musical audition, and the interview. It shows actors how to see their performance through the eyes of prospective employers, how to sell themselves even before they step into character, and how to interpret roles without outside direction.

Performing Arts/Theater/0-679-73228-4

A PRACTICAL HANDBOOK FOR THE ACTOR
by Melissa Bruder

A Practical Handbook for the Actor is a simple and essential book about the craft of acting, which describes a technique developed by the authors in their work with Pulitzer Prize–winning playwright David Mamet, actor W. H. Macy, and director Gregory Mosher. It is written for any actor who has ever experienced the frustrations of acting classes that lacked clarity and objectivity and that failed to provide a dependable set of tools. An actor's job, the author's state, is to "find a way to live truthfully under the imaginary circumstances of the play."

Theater/0-394-74412-8

TRUE AND FALSE
Heresy and Common Sense for the Actor
by David Mamet

Invent nothing, deny nothing, speak up, stand up, stay out of school. With these words one of our brilliantly iconoclastic playwrights takes on the art and profession of professional acting. From acting schools, "interpretation," "sense memory," and "The Method," Mamet takes a jackhammer to the idols of contemporary acting, while revealing the true heroism and nobility of the craft. He shows actors how to undertake auditions and rehearsals, deal with agents and directors, engage audiences, and stay faithful to the script, while rejecting the temptations that seduce so many of their colleagues.

Theater/Acting/0-679-77264-2

AN ACROBAT OF THE HEART
A Physical Approach to Acting Inspired
by the Work of Jerzy Grotowski
by Stephen Wangh

In *An Acrobat of the Heart*, teacher-director-playwright Stephen Wangh reveals how Jerzy Grotowski's physical exercises can open a pathway to the actor's inner creativity. Drawing on Grotowski's insights and on the work of Stanislavsky, Uta Hagen, and others, Wangh bridges the gaps between rigorous physical training, practical scene, and character technique. Wangh's students give descriptions of their struggles and breakthroughs, demonstrating how to transform these remarkable lessons into a personal journey of artistic growth.

Theater/Acting Technique/0-375-70672-0

AUDITIONING
An Actor-Friendly Guide
by Joanna Merlin

Theater veteran and acting teacher Joanna Merlin has written the definitive guide to auditioning for stage and screen, bringing to it a valuable dual perspective. In this highly informative and accessible book, Merlin provides everything the actor needs to achieve self-confidence and artistic honesty—from the most basic practical tips to an in-depth framework for preparing a part. Filled with advice from the most esteemed people in the business, such as James Lapine, Nora Ephron, and Stephen Sondheim, this indispensable resource will arm the reader to face an actor's greatest challenge: getting the part.

Theater/Acting/0-375-72537-7

STELLA ADLER ON IBSEN, STRINDBERG, AND CHEKHOV
by Stella Adler, edited by Barry Paris

As a Stanislavsky disciple and founder of her own highly esteemed acting conservatory, Stella Adler was both an actress and an eminent acting teacher, training her students—among them Marlon Brando, Al Pacino, and Robert DeNiro—in the art of script interpretation. The classic lectures collected here, delivered over a period of forty years, bring to life the plays of the three fathers of modern drama: Henrik Ibsen, August Strindberg, and Anton Chekhov. With passionate conviction and shrewd insight, Adler explains how their plays forever changed the world of dramaturgy while offering enduring insights on society, class, culture, and the role of the actor.

Theater/0-679-74698-6